Life of a Windsor War Baby

Stewart Hughes

First Published 2000

Published by
Stewart Hughes
Eton Wick
Berkshire

© Stewart Hughes, 2000

ISBN No: 0-9537800-0-7

All rights reserved. No part of this book may be reproduced or transmitted in any form, or by any means, electronically or mechanically, including photocopying, fax, recording or by any information retrieval system, without prior permission from the copyright holder.

Printed by Thameslink Ltd
www.thamesweb.co.uk/books/
Windsor (01753) 620540

Front cover illustrations
The Chase, The Convent (Hatch Lane), Two Evacuees,
Windsor Castle, Windsor Central Station

Back cover Illustrations
Aerial view in early 1900s

Dedication

This book is dedicated to my wife Grace, without whose patience and understanding it would not have been possible.

Acknowledgements

I would like to thank my wife Grace who kindly proof read my original text, also my son, Andrew for his excellent photographic and computer work. Without the help of these two people, I would not have been able to complete this book.

I would also like to thank the following people:

- Mrs Judith Hunter BSc PhD (Royal Borough Collection) for her advice and help on the way forward.
- Mother Jane Olive (Reverend Mother Superior at the Convent of St John the Baptist in Windsor) for her permission for her permission to use photographs from the Convent's book 'A Joyous Service'.
- Mrs Beryl Hedges for permission to use photographs from her private collection.
- Patricia Curtis (Windsor Reference Library)
- Mr G Cullingham (Windsor Local History Publications Group).
- Mr N I Hamilton (Manager of External Affairs, Slough Estates) for permission to use photographs from the book 'Long Lease'.
- Sue Healy (museum curator at the Thames Valley Police training Centre).
- Museum of Docklands Projects, London
- Eileen Gallagher (King Edward VII Hospital, Windsor)
- Mr J Lennox & Mr Ken Kirtland (Windsor Liberal Club)
- Mrs Freda Mason (Theatre Royal Windsor)
- Mr Peter Knibbs (Windsor Sea Cadets)
- Mr Dronsfield & Mr Linn (Windsor Housing Association)
- Harrow School
- Mr Wilson (Clerk of Works, Windsor Castle)
- Mr Morfit (Head of member Services, Windsor Borough Council
- Slough Reference Library
- Sabina Sutherland (Berkshire Records Office)
- Penny Hatfield (Eton College Archivist)
- Christine Vickers (Eton College Photographic Archivist)
- Gordon Rogers (Collector's Choice)

I would like to give my sincere thanks to all the people and organisations for the help they gave me while researching and writing this book. My apologies are tendered for any inadvertent omissions in attribution. I have made every effort to establish copyright where required and to obtain permission to reproduce, but if I have inadvertently omitted to do so in the case of any particular photograph, I offer my sincere apologies.

STOKE PLACE

**Residential Conference Centre
01753 534790**

Contents

Acknowledgements — iv

Changed Local Names — vii

Illustrations — viii

Map Index c. 1945 — x

Ward Royal 1968 — xi

Preface — xii

Chapter One - The Early Years — 13

Chapter Two - An Impressionable Age — 27

Chapter Three - Work And Play — 33

Chapter Four - Changing Lifestyles — 44

Chapter Five - Dideorde Manor — 54

Chapter Six – The Teenage Years — 63

Chapter Seven - A Walk Through Town — 71

Chapter Eight - The Lean Years — 85

Changed Local Names

Local names that have changed over the years

Original Name	Now Known As
Wolf Public House	The Maypole
Olde House Hotel	Sir Christopher Wren's House
Old Infirmary	Windsor Liberal Club
New Road	Clarence Road
Pitt's Field	The Acre
Goods Yards	Coach Park
Bier Lane	River Street

Illustrations

Map Index. c. 1945 x
Ward Royal 1968 xi
The V1 Pilotless Monoplane (DoodleBug) xii
Windsor Castle from The Brocas 14
Windsor Road Bridge early in the century 16
Windsor Road Bridge now Pedestrianised 16
The Burning Bush outside the College Hall 17
Burning Bush - A close up 17
A house at Timber Town 19
Entrance to Slough Estate in the '40s 20
Entrance to the Slough Estate in 1999 20
Slough High Street circa 1930 21
Crown Hotel Slough circa 1930 21
Workers arrive at the station on Slough Estate 22
Slough Trading Co. first headquarters 22
The Old Police and Fire Station 24
New Police Station 25
New Fire Station 25
Alexander Road Infants School site 29
A charabanc ready to depart outside the Noah's Ark PH 31
Victoria Street Alms Houses 34
Sir Christopher Wren's House Hotel as it is today. 34
The gateway, new Barrack building 36
The Dispensary, Church St 37
The Dispensary, Church St today 37
The old Infirmary and Dispensary building 38
The new complex built on the site of the old Infirmary. 38
King Edward VII Hospital 39
King Edward VII Hospital undergoing renovation today 39
Windsor Liberal Rifle Club team, 1950s 40

The Old Graveyard and Madeira Walk	40
Windsor Liberal Club in the late 1940's.	42
Late Victorian terraced house, Adelaide Square	45
Grandfather Bench, Constable No. 17, in 1909.	46
The Gasworks Yard during the 1947 floods	47
Bier Lane (River Street) in the mid 1800s	50
River Street after the Italienne Quarter was demolished	51
River Street car park as it is today	51
Clewer Houses of Mercy Laundry	52
The Sister's Garden	52
Haymaking in the 30s	53
The old Royal Free School building	55
New Lodge at Winkfield	56
The Copper Horse, Snow Hill	58
Aboard the Royal Daffodil	59
Windsor and Eton Riverside Station	60
The Three Elms Public House	64
Windsor Sea Cadets circa 1905	65
Aboard HMS Dido	66
Group in front of a float, Windsor Carnival	67
Athens	72
The inscription on the Athens Memorial Stone	72
River Street (Bier Lane)	73
The drinking trough, the Hundred Steps	76
Oxford Road before Ward Royal was built	78
Oxford Road now	78
Peascod Street in the early 1900s	80
Peascod Street in the late 1990s	80
Star and Garter Hotel	81
Three shops that replaced the Star and Garter Hotel.	82
Statue of Queen Victoria	84
Ration Books - a must for everyone	88

Map Index. c. 1945

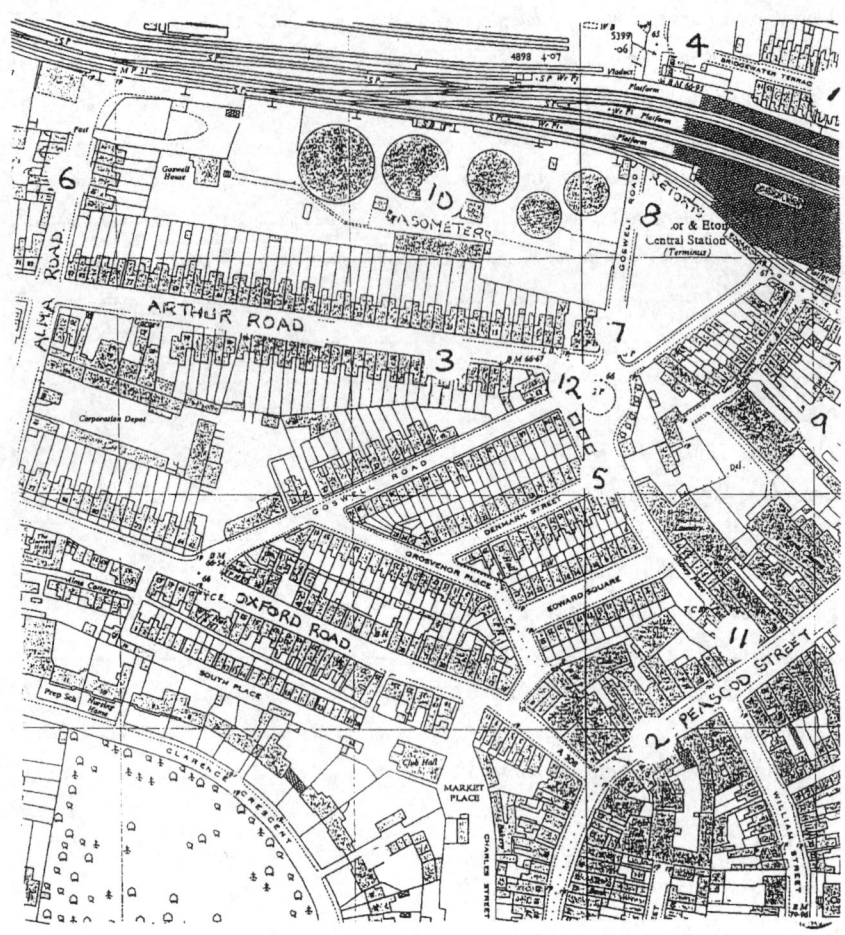

1 Bridgewater Terrace
2 Peascod Street
3 10 Arthur Road
4 Tolladay Cottages
5 Air Raid Shelters
6 Sir Sydney Camm's Birthplace
7 Noah's Ark Public House
8 Retorts
9 Windsor & Eton Dairy Depot
10 Gasometers
11 Footpath
12 Vettise's Shop

Ward Royal 1968

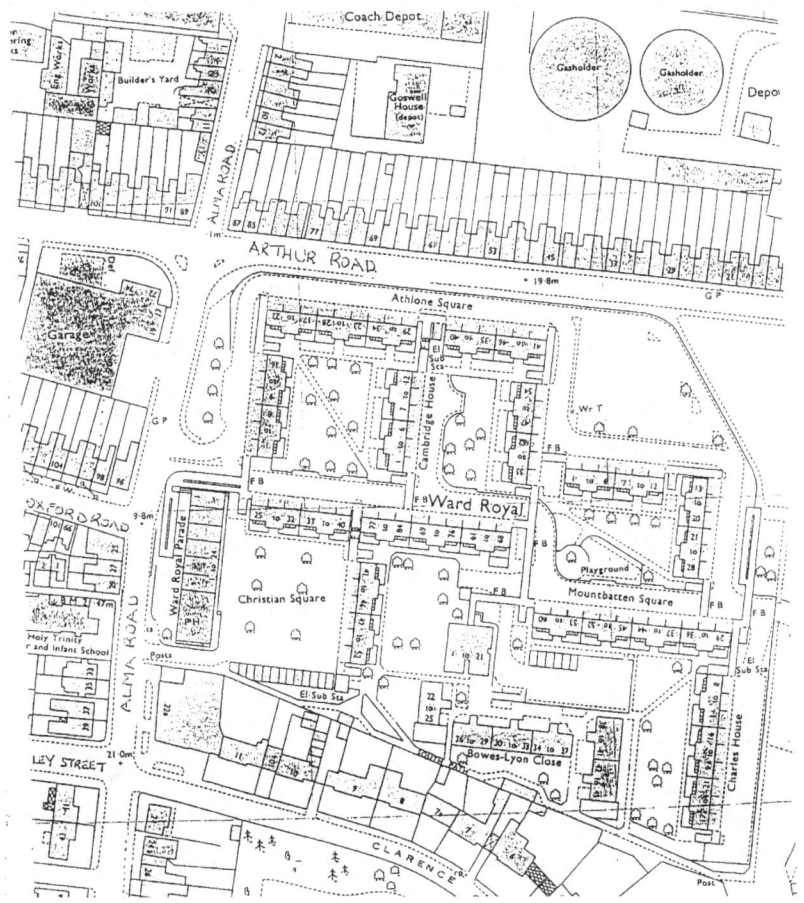

The "Ward Royal" complex was built in 1966 and first let in 1968. It is situated with Arthur Road to the north and consists of 236 one, two, and three bedroom flats. The "King Edward Court" shopping complex lies to the south of the railway viaduct and is linked to "Ward Royal" by a footbridge. Both of these developments replaced many streets of terraced houses clustered around the gasworks and goods yard. The close knit community that had lived there for many years was re-housed in new accommodation in and around Windsor.

Preface

War is a subject that has been well documented over the years. This book is not about war itself, but the effect it has on the population, the drastic changes it makes to peoples lives, and their attitude to life itself.

My story begins in a small English town with a population of just over twenty thousand. Windsor Castle dominates the main shopping centre and the riverside below. It is a magnificent fortress built on a chalky outcrop. On a clear day, from the Round Tower at the centre of the castle, panoramic views of seven counties can be seen.

It started out many centuries ago as a simple motte and bailey. Over the years it has been added to, altered and partially destroyed by fire more than once, but it has survived. It is now the largest inhabited castle in the world.

During the late thirties, the talk and threat of war became a reality. On 3rd September 1939 at midday the world learned that Great Britain was at war with Germany. This was a devastating blow to the hopes and aspirations of the people in this green and pleasant land. The map of the world showed large areas coloured pink, and the Royal Navy ruled the waves, but soon this was all to change.

Through the centuries these small islands had been plundered by seafarers from afar, some that raped and pillaged, others who settled and intermarried and in turn defended their new homeland. It was through this process that a strong, determined but fair-minded nation evolved. The resourcefulness of these people was to come to bear during the next five years.

This period in history proved to be the most turbulent and devastating the world had ever known. Great Britain would never be the same again.

The parents of the 'War Babies' had hopes and plans for the future, but it was to prove to be a difficult time. This island home was to change out of all recognition during the coming years.

In this book I have attempted to portray the type of childhood that was taken for granted by the youngsters of the forties and fifties of the twentieth century.

Chapter One - The Early Years

I was born in 1939 in a terraced house just yards from the local gas works. My parents were of Victorian upbringing, which certainly reflected on the strict way in which I was raised. On many occasions I considered this unfair and totally unnecessary, and during my teenage years there were a few conflicts between their totalitarian ideas and my thoughts on how things should be. Looking back though, it really did me no harm, and has stood me in good stead during the upbringing of my own children and considering today's liberal attitudes especially, it has proved to be a godsend.

My father was a carpenter and joiner and attended night school while learning his trade. Methods of production in my early years were beginning to change, and mass produced goods were edging the craftsman away from his chosen trade. Machines gradually replaced the skills learned and passed on by previous generations as the demand for goods increased. This situation was aggravated by the onset of World War II when more and more of everything needed to be produced at an alarming rate.

The men who did not volunteer, or who were not called up, were used in the war effort at home. For many years my father worked in a factory making packing cases for aircraft parts. During the post-war years, to a certain extent, the craftsman came into his own again as life started to return to normal, but the war had changed many things and mass production was the way forward.

When my father passed away in 1974, he still had a full set of craftsman's tools, all slotted in their rightful places in a workbox that he had painstakingly constructed as a young man. The thing I remember most clearly about it was a set of twenty-seven planes used for general and specialist work. I passed them on to a company he used to work for. Many of them had no use in the modern workshop, but were put on show as a reminder to the workforce of the day of how things used to be. The box, no longer used for tools, has travelled everywhere with me. With the shelving removed and a little modification it became a toy box for my own children. Later, a padded top was added so that it could be used as an ottoman and it is now used as storage for the Christmas tree and decorations.

My mother was one of four children whose own mother had died when she was only ten years old. A strict father and a stepmother who acted more like a housekeeper raised them. They lived in a Victorian style terraced house in the upmarket part of Windsor called Adelaide Square. The mixture of my mother's upbringing and the fact that my father was an illegitimate

Windsor Castle from The Brocas

child (a fact carefully hidden in those days) was probably part of the reason for my rigid upbringing.

Strangely enough though, when I was ten, my mother went out to work as a canteen assistant (or dinner lady as they were affectionately known in those days). At the time it was still looked down upon if your mother went out to work. A woman's place had always been in the home, but this was one effect that the war had on the lives of the British people. I must give credit to my parents. I was never a 'latch key kid' and my mother was always there when I got home from school and during the school holidays.

My memories of the start of the war, because of my young age, are a little hazy, but one or two incidents are indelibly imprinted on my mind. It is with these memories, together with small amounts of information that my parents passed on to me, I am able to start my story of 'The Life of a Windsor War Baby'.

Windsor and the surrounding area was not too badly damaged when compared with other parts of the country. It was thought that Mr Hitler rather fancied the Castle for himself and therefore deliberately avoided it with the bombing raids from Germany. On many occasions, the enemies' navigators found the huge Castle a convenient landmark, and they could then follow the river to their main target, London. Perhaps he was not aware that the Slough Trading Estate (the name by which it is known today) was only a mile away, although I doubt it. It was here that valuable war work was carried out, along with the Hawker Aircraft Co., a stone's throw away at Langley. Both could have been prime targets for any bomber crew. At its peak, the Langley factory was turning out five aircraft per day but it was the demoralisation of the people of London that seemed to be the main goal. Perhaps it was the very successful barrage balloon, a marvellous invention with it's steel hawser below, that could have been the deterrent, as no pilot would relish the thought of hitting one of those.

A bomb did drop on the goods yard at Windsor, now the coach park next to Alexandra Gardens. It made a direct hit on a goods wagon belonging to the Co-Op, blasting it to pieces and destroying part of the Tolladay Cottage which used to stand on the corner of Bridgewater Terrace, opposite Alexandra Gardens. The only legible piece of evidence of what had been hit was the number plate of the wagon found amongst the rubble of the cottage. Another bomb fell at the back of Dysons the Jewellers in Thames Street, which was directly opposite the Curfew Tower in Windsor Castle. In later years, the shop became famous for its clock in the pavement, but alas, neither are still there now. A round steel plate still covers the hole where the clock used to be. What a different story it would have been if the bombs had dropped a few hundred yards away on the Gasworks which were situated on the other side of the railway viaduct where the gasometers there were full of highly inflammable gas.

These incidents during the war are those that my parents have passed on to me, but I do remember part of the goods wagon incident. The siren had woken me, and as my mother put her hand on the light switch of the front room where I had been sleeping, the blast from the bomb knocked her against the opposite wall. Another incident involved a V1 rocket plane, better known as a Doodlebug (a name given to it by the RAF). This one hit the dust constructor chimney at the Council depot off Kentons Lane at Dedworth. It was a sunny summers day in 1944 and my mother had taken me shopping. We were in a shop called William Creeks in Peascod Street, situated opposite where the new Post Office now stands. The siren had sounded, and the unmistakable sound of a Doodlebug rocket engine was heard, followed by that deathly silence when it ran out of fuel. It was now nose-diving towards the Earth. Very shortly afterwards, there was an explosion and again silence, followed by the welcome sound of the all clear siren.

The Trading Estate gave work to a large number of people from Windsor and the surrounding areas. The Windsor Relief Road (A332) had not even been conceived and all of the traffic heading for Slough and London (including double-decker buses) used the Windsor River Bridge to Eton, passing through the narrow high street and on to the College. This stop was known as the Burning Bush, the name given to an ornate lamp standard that still stands there, although it has now been moved onto the wide pavement

Windsor Road Bridge early in the century

Windsor Road Bridge now Pedestrianised

The Burning Bush was in the middle of the road in front of Cannon Yard at Eton College. It is now on the wide pavement outside the College Hall and Library

A close up showing some of the ornate iron work on the Burning Bush street lamp

outside the College Hall and library. The original position was in the middle of the road where Common Lane meets the Slough Road (B3022). This road then continues between the old school buildings. On the left is a field called Sixpenny on the far side of which the old Five Courts used to stand.

On the right hand side behind the brick wall is where the infamous Eton Wall Game is played. As the road goes over the Fifteen Arch Bridge, under which Colenorton Brook runs, and still looking to the right, is a pool of water called Ellows Pond. Jutting out into the water is a piece of land called the Leg of Mutton, which takes its name from the shape. The brook then enters the Thames below Romney Weir. The road continues past Willow Brook on the left and continues until it reaches the Crown Corner at Slough.

Many of the workforce used to cycle this journey twice daily, whatever the weather and many of those who lived at Spital or Dedworth needed to travel to central Windsor first in order to use the river crossing. The nearest other road bridge was at Maidenhead, six miles away, or via Datchet, quite a considerable detour. With the additional mile from the Crown Corner to the Estate, those who lived on the outskirts of Windsor had about a four-mile ride each way.

Travelling on the top deck of a bus, and meeting another bus coming in the other direction while crossing the river bridge could be an unnerving experience. The bridge is so narrow, and peering down into the fast flowing River Thames from that height could be quite scary.

The Slough Trading Company was formed by a group of businessmen. The 800 acres of land had previously been compulsorily purchased from an estate known as Cippenham Court by the government for the storage of old and broken military vehicles from the First World War. This company repaired and sold these now redundant vehicles, with those that were beyond repair being sold for scrap. By 1924 most of the stock had been cleared. Slough Trading Co. now erected buildings on the land and leased them to manufacturers. Slough Estates was born. It is known today as the Trading Estate or, by those a little more advanced in years, The Dump (for obvious reasons).

Some of the first companies to rent these premises are now household names, such as Gillette, Citroen Cars, Johnson & Johnson and Mars to name but a few. Timber Town, as it was known, was built to house the workers who had come to the area to find work. A large number came from Wales, and the community that grew there became known as New South Wales. At one time, this accommodation was also used to house prisoners of war, and was situated on the opposite side of the Farnham Road (A355) to the Estate approximately where Manor park is now situated. In 1942 the Estate boasted 422 factories and workshops employing 40,000 workers, a lot of which had been converted to produce much-needed products for the war. Mars had

A House at Timber Town

been one of the later companies to arrive on the Estate and therefore should have been one of the first to be converted, but as every food pack for the military contained chocolate, part of the factory was allowed to continue producing it. Other parts of the same building were used for canning bacon and motorcycle production and repairs. Both of these companies had been bombed out in London and had been re-established at Slough.

The Estate was fast becoming vulnerable to air raids. In one building alone, no less than 10,000 incendiary bombs were in various stages of production at any one time. To try and ensure protection from the air, barrage balloons were used to deter aircraft. Also, large candle like structures were placed every twenty yards with chimneys on top. When the enemy planes dropped flares so that photographs could be taken, Italian prisoners of war were used to light oil-soaked rags inside these structures, creating a thick smoke screen above the Estate. This shrouded the view from the air, and although the enemy knew that there was something of importance there, they didn't know exactly what. Even if this system was not completely successful in confusing the Germans, it most certainly choked the workers below!

Entrance to the Estate in the '40s from the Bath Road (A4)

Entrance to the Estate in 1999 from the Bath Road (A4)

Slough High Street circa 1930 Looking towards The Crown Corner

Crown Hotel Slough circa 1930

Workers arrive at the station on the Estate courtesy of GWR

Slough Trading Co. first headquarters in Bedford Avenue

High Duty Alloys was directly hit by an incendiary bomb, which in turn set off an explosion killing six and injuring forty and stopping production for a short while. The overworked power station was surrounded by a high wire fence and was guarded twenty-four hours a day. This was not to defend it from air attack, but from ground attack by the IRA.

As part of the defence of the Estate, a mock village of wooden huts, kept lit at night, was built at the bend in the river at Datchet. This decoy village was directly in line with the Estate, much to the horror of the people who lived in sleepy old Datchet village at the time.

> Come friendly bombs fall on Slough
> It isn't fit for humans now
> There isn't grass to graze a cow
> Swarm over death
> Come bombs and blow to smithereens
> These air conditioned bright canteens
> Tinned fruit, tinned meat, tinned milk, tinned beans
> Tinned minds, tinned breath
> Mess up the mess they call a town
> A home for ninety seven down
> And once a week half a crown
> For twenty Years
> Sir John Betjemen – Poet Laureate 1972-84

The Windsor Borough Police were formed in 1856 and operated under that name until 1947 when it amalgamated and became the Berkshire Constabulary. During the Second World War, the Borough Police consisted of 45 men and was assisted by the newly formed Special Constables. These 113 men worked alongside the regulars, together with the Home Guard who were formed in 1940. These three organisations worked together giving as much protection as possible to citizens and property in the Windsor area. The main concern in the early days of the war was that an invasion was imminent. The Home Guard was made up of people from all walks of life. Some were veterans from the 1914/18 War. The age limit was supposed to be sixty-five but some members were a little liberal with the truth when enrolling at the Police Station in St Leonards Road. The western defences of the town were in Smiths Lane, near the Wolf Public House (now known as The Maypole). The Home Guard's headquarters was at the Drill Hall St Catherine's Church, a few yards walk from the Three Elms Public House on the corner of Hatch Lane. Some of the patrols managed to cover an area which contained six or seven drinking establishments which, of course, they were obliged to visit to ensure all was well, before returning to headquarters. I can remember the reinforced concrete Pillbox at the Elms Crossroads. It stood there for years after the war had ended.

The Old Police and Fire Station in St Leonards Road. Built 1906

My father was a member of the Specials. I remember him telling me that during one particular blackout, a light was showing at the back of one of the big houses in Park Street that overlooked the Long Walk. It came from a small window at the very top. He had to crawl along a ledge four stories up and break in and switch it off before it was shot out by the artillery positioned nearby. In a darkened town, one light would have been a beacon for enemy aircraft.

The air raid shelters for Arthur Road were just around the corner by Vatises shop, between Goswell Road and Denmark Street. When the siren sounded at night, our family used to crowd into the space under the stairs for added protection. If you were caught out in the street, the nearest communal shelter was used if there was room. One day I was being taken back to the infants school in Alexandra Road by my mother. We had just about reached the site of the new Post Office yard in William Street when the siren sounded. I can remember my mother hesitating, not knowing whether it was better to hurry on to the school and it's shelter, or to the one by Vatises, the distance being about the same. This was the first recollection I have of the hairs on the back of my neck standing on end. I had sensed the fear of being caught out in the open emanating from my mother.

Not long before the D-Day landings, there were a lot of troop movements, and much to the delight of the children who lived along Arthur Road, the

New Police Station in Alma Road

New Fire Station in St Marks Road

The V1 Pilotless Monoplane (DoodleBug)
25ft Long, constructed of plywood and sheet steel.
The nose was armed with 850kg of high explosive

convoys passed their front doors. We waved and cheered, and in response the Americans waved back and threw us real American chewing gum. I often wonder now just how many of those young men returned to their loved ones back home.

Between 1942 and 1945 there was an American Air Force camp at Smiths Lawn, now known as the Polo Ground. It consisted of twenty-five men living in tented accommodation and fourteen Dakota aircraft. The American airmen were often seen about Windsor. Later the camp became an RAF Tiger Moth training camp.

In 1940/41 supplies of raw materials was running low, this being due to the heavy losses sustained by the sea convoys. As part of the war effort, iron railings were removed from gardens and parks, loaded onto a barge and sent downstream. I understand that this barge was later bombed and sank with it's cargo on board.

An all too familiar site around the town was the Telegraph Boy, and in those dark days of the war, everyone hoped that it was not their house that he propped his bicycle up against. When the rat-a-tat-tat was heard on the door, everyone waited with baited breath hoping that the telegram would not start "It is with deepest regret...." One felt so helpless on such occasions.

> The kiss of the sun for pardon
> The song of the birds for mirth
> You are nearer God's heart in a garden
> Than anywhere else on Earth
> Dorothy Frances Gurney

Chapter Two - An Impressionable Age

The celebrations at the end of the war were over, but the euphoria that they had created was still very evident. This gave the people a new perspective on life. Much had been lost and a whole way of life destroyed. New ideas were mixed up with old, but slowly a new way of life began to take shape. Plans for the future were being made, and peacetime Britain was on the move again.

Raw materials were in short supply and food was still rationed. There was also a shortage of able-bodied men. The death toll from the war was horrendous, and many more were injured or disabled for life. I was six years old now and, as youngsters do, I soon forgot about the bad times and got on with growing up.

In the garden in Arthur Road, there was a large rambling Honeysuckle bush. It had spread all over the0 outside toilet wall. My mother allowed me to pick some leaves to be used as a vegetable to be served with Sunday lunch. I actually saw the leaves boiling in a pan on the stove. I don't know how long it was before I realised that they had been substituted with cabbage that my father had grown. This meal always tasted smashing though!

The variety of food available during the post-war years was fairly limited, but the luxury goods that were available before the war were slowly starting to appear. I had never tasted, or even seen a banana. One day, after being met from school, I was told that there was a treat for me when I got home. Needless to say, I nagged and nagged and even before we had left Alexander Road I was allowed my first taste. I think that my mother was as keen to taste them again as I was for the first time. I didn't really like them to start with, but as time passed, I acquired the taste. To this day, a portion of banana custard, especially cold, goes down very well.

The highlight of the day at infant school was the gill of milk issued as a compulsory measure to ensure that all youngsters got some vitamins. The milk was in small, squat, wide-necked bottles with a cardboard lid printed with the word 'PRESS' where the straw was to be inserted. The downside to the day at school was the portion of halibut orange that was issued. I hated it so much that I can remember the taste to this day and the exact spot from where it used to be issued and the lingering aftertaste.

During one of the school lessons, we were given a loose weave piece of cloth and told to shred it to pieces. What the benefit of this particular activity was, I will never know. I was forced to hold any writing implement with my right hand, which I found very difficult. At one stage during those early years, it became apparent that by forcing a naturally left-handed child to be right handed caused more harm than good. The rules must have been changed because all of a sudden I was taught to use my left hand. To this day, the only task I do completely with my right hand is to use a pair of scissors.

Being inquisitive, as little boys are, I was forever asking questions and responding to the answers with "Why?" I suppose that on such occasions mothers do get fed up with their offspring. In one unguarded moment, when asked why roads were higher in the middle than at the sides, she answered "It's where they bury fat people". Well, this puzzled me for a long while, until one day when it dawned on me that there were more roads than there were fat people, therefore this could not be right. I was already aware that when somebody passed on they were buried shortly afterwards, and anyway, I had not seen them keep digging up the road.

Up to the age of about nine years, I suppose the term for me would have been 'a sickly child'. The doctor assured my parents that I would grow out of the bilious attacks caused by excess acid in my system. It was inconvenient, to say the least, being ill every few weeks.

On one such occasion, I was recuperating in bed after a bad turn. I was playing a game of Bagatelle that my father had made for me. Although I had been warned not to keep the spare steel ball bearing in my mouth, I did and the inevitable happened and it slid down my throat. I shouted for my mother and told her what had happened, but in disbelief she started to search the bedclothes and my pyjamas, but alas, to no avail. After counting the ball bearings and realising that one was actually missing, she shouted for my aunt who was downstairs at the time. Between them, I was turned upside down, hung by my ankles and thumped hard on the back while being vigorously shaken. Suddenly, the ball bearing shot out of my mouth, rolled across the linoleum, and stopped in the corner of the bedroom. As quickly as the crisis had arisen, it was over, thanks to the quick actions of my mother and aunt. I don't ever remember seeing that game of Bagatelle again. As for the bilious attacks, they seemed to clear up after that. Perhaps it was the shock.

Christmas was always a good time, even during the years of austerity that followed the war. One present that I can remember in particular was a wooden battleship painted grey that my father had made for me. It was constructed of about seven or eight pieces that fitted together very precisely on a wooden hull. It was difficult to see that it came to pieces and was not a solid object. On one side, just below the Plimsoll line was a wooden button. When pressed, it would set off a mousetrap inside the hull and the superstructure exploded. I must have had a very caring father as he was always making me things, although at the time it was not fully appreciated. Another present that he made me, this time for my birthday, was a kite. It was as tall as me, which meant that I had to be accompanied when I went to

Alexander Road Infants School site – some of the school buildings have been incorporated into the private dwellings and the school playground is now landscaped with parking bays

fly it. On it's maiden flight, it nose-dived into the ground and broke it two. What a shame after all that time and effort spent making it. Perhaps my father should have stuck to shipbuilding rather than branching out into aeronautics.

I was the envy of all the other kids in Arthur Road when my father made me a wooden scooter with a press down brake on the rear wheel. Shop bought ones were very expensive and not very strong at all.

I was getting to the age when boys often helped (or hindered) the local deliveryman. It was just for fun, but occasionally you might get a little treat. The roads were fairly safe, as not many working folk owned a car. Traffic consisted mainly of trades vehicles, often horse drawn, and bicycles. It was fairly safe to play in the street, even though it was a main road. It was a common sight to see people's front and back doors open all day, especially in the summertime, without fear of being robbed or mugged. One day, a prisoner of war escaped. He ran along Arthur road, in through an open front door, out through the back door, down the garden and over the wall into Goswell Road before disappearing. I never did find out whether he was recaptured or not.

One of the disadvantages of an old terraced house was that of only having an outside toilet, especially in the winter. There were no en-suite facilities or central heating, and with a toilet door that did not fit properly, going to the loo could be a cold and draughty experience. A bedpan (or gasunder) was often the order of the day, or rather, the night. Early one summer's morning I had run outside to use the toilet while still in my pyjamas. I tugged at the drawstring and caught my unmentionable in the knot. I screamed the place down. My mother came running and managed to calm me down, as mothers have a knack of doing. She managed to untie the drawstring without any damage to my pride, or me.

Most people who were lucky enough to have a garden grew their own vegetables. If you could afford the rent on an allotment it was even better. My father kept a vegetable patch at Arthur Road. On one particular occasion, a rake that had been propped up against the wall had fallen over, prong side up. I fell over it and pierced my wrist on one of the upturned prongs. I still bear the scar today. I don't remember the outcome except for a good telling off for playing in the garden, and not in the yard as I had been told to do.

Stuffed marrow was a meal frequently served in our house. I could never understand how the first marrow of the season always had my name engraved on it in large letters (clever people, these fathers). Even now when I am gardening I always lay the tools in a wheelbarrow or put them away immediately. A lesson learnt early in life.

Horse-drawn vehicles often delivered milk and coal. The trademark left behind by these animals was a much sought after commodity for gardens and allotments, so someone was usually quickly out there with a shovel and bucket. I regularly helped the milkman out on his round and sometimes went with him to the depot off Goswell Lane. His name was Bill, and if my luck was really in, he would bring me some new cardboard milk bottle tops. These were used for a game called Flicksies that was played against a wall. Collecting cigarette cards and matchboxes were also common hobbies amongst the kids. I found the unused milk bottle tops were good for bartering when the popular pastime of Swapsies was in progress.

My aunt Ede lived in a flat above our elderly neighbour, who was a severe asthmatic and was confined to the ground floor. She was a tall lady who had apparently taken a shine to me as she was a spinster with no children of her own. Consequently she rather spoilt me. One day, for some reason best known to herself, as I was about to go out to play, she dabbed some perfume behind one of my ears. I went out to play at the corner shop, Vatises. Johnny, their son, and I were playing in their back yard where a batch of genuine 'Italian' ice cream was being made. There was always a nice sweet smell in

A Charabanc ready to depart outside the Noah's Ark earlier in the century (possibly the late twenties)

the yard, and with the added smell of the perfume, I was stung by, a bee. Funny how you can go off aunts (for a while, anyway) and I certainly did not want to be called a sissy, so I steered clear whenever makeup was around after that.

The landlord of a pub called the Noah's Ark, on the corner of Arthur Road and opposite Vatises shop, was a real local character. His name was Jim Osbourne, an ex-military man of means. He was a gambling gent and was always very smartly dressed, with a fresh flower in his buttonhole every day. The pub had two bars; the working men from the gasworks opposite used the public bar. They used to gather for a well-earned pint or two after a long hot shift in front of the retorts. The saloon bar was where the occasional lady could be found accompanied by her spouse or fiancé. There was also a small room called 'The Snug', which was only large enough for two people (and was even overcrowded then). The only door to it opened directly on to the pavement outside. It was from there that jugs or pots of beer could be purchased for home consumption. My parents were friends of the landlord and his good lady, and when he took my mother over for a drink, I was put in the back room to play cards with their daughter and her cousin. A game of snap or patience was about all we were allowed to play. My, how things have changed!

While researching this book, the old pub building, which has stood empty for a while has become derelict, and has been pulled down. The first eight houses along Arthur Road have also been demolished. This was to make way for a new office block with public and private parking, currently being built on the old site of the gasworks and the adjoining goods yards.

One of my last memories of living in Arthur Road was a trip that my mother took me on to the airport at Heathrow. We travelled by 'Green Line' coach from Windsor to a point on the Bath Road (A4) called Northside. It was from here that trips around the airport were possible. These were made sitting on an open trailer fitted with wooden bench type seats and towed by a tractor type vehicle. These trips lasted about three-quarters of an hour and even crossed the runway. Mind you, in those days, aircraft movement could be hours apart, and if you were lucky, you might even see two moving aircraft on one trip! I have tried to trace the company who organised these trips so that I could refresh my memory with more details, but to date I have not succeeded. This was a time that the three London airports between them boasted 47 aircraft movements per day.

Chapter Three - Work And Play

My parents believed that a child should be taught the value of money, and that it had to be earned. When I was taken to see my grandmother, who lived in the Alms Houses opposite the old Victoria Barracks in Victoria Street, one of my jobs was to take the empty accumulator to a shop called Fullers, next to the barracks' entrance. It was to be exchanged for a recharged one, for which a small fee was payable. It would then last another week before it ran low again. They were cumbersome things, and quite heavy for a little boy to carry, a far cry from the minuscule power packs available today, but it gave my grandmother the use of her radio set for another week. Another of my tasks was to collect the coke for the fires in the house at Arthur Road from the gasworks. My father had made a barrow especially for the job. This was usually the last task on a Saturday morning before setting off for the 'ABC Minors' show at the Playhouse Cinema. This stood opposite Sir Christopher Wren's House in Thames Street. It has since been pulled down and replaced with a modern office block.

The Saturday Morning Pictures, as they were affectionately known, were always very popular. For the equivalent of two and a half pence in today's money, there was a good two hours entertainment. If it happened to be your birthday, your name was read out and you were called up onto the stage. The whole audience then sang the Happy Birthday song to you, followed by the Minor's own song. The show usually consisted of a Roy Rogers type western preceded by a couple of cartoons. On special occasions, a local comedian or magician gave a live performance. Before the show, popular tunes of the day were played on the cinema organ, which was situated in a pit immediately in front of the stage.

> ABC Minor's Song
> We are the boys and girls well known as
> The minors of the ABC
> And every Saturday all line up
> To see the films we like and shout aloud with glee
> We like to laugh and have a sing song
> Just a happy crowd are we
> We're all pals together
> We're the minors of the ABC

In Goswell Road there was a cobbler called Mr Neale who worked from a shed behind his terraced house. To get to his workshop, it was necessary to walk through the house and into the garden. It used to take me a while to

Victoria Street Alms Houses

Sir Christopher Wren's House Hotel as it is today.
It was previously known as the Old House Hotel

complete this errand, as he used to let me stay and watch him work. I was fascinated by the method he used, keeping the nails and tacks in his mouth, and taking them out one at a time with such speed and accuracy. With a quick tap, tap, tap of the hammer, each one would go into the right place around the heel or sole, and with such precision. It was no wonder that shoes lasted so long in those days, when compared with the three or four staples from a gun used by the 'While U Wait' shops today.

During the school holidays, when playing with some chums who lived in the Barracks, I used to try and sneak past the gate guard, especially if he had gone into the guardroom to answer the phone, or was busy taking the details of an incoming lorry. Of course, the Barracks were strictly out of bounds to children of non-military parents. The soldiers on duty were usually wise to the trick of the 'Town Kids', as we were known. There was the odd occasion when I managed to get in and play for a couple of hours, but then suddenly I would be looking up into the stern face of the Sergeant Major. Without hesitation, I was escorted to the main gate by my ear, and shouted at in a loud voice to 'Scram and don't come back, or I'll kick your *ss for you'.

Another of my school holiday pastimes was to go to Creek's store in Peascod Street. This store had an overhead spring-loaded shuttle. When a purchase was made at the counter, your money was loaded into the shuttle pod and propelled along a wire to the glass-fronted office above the sales floor. A few moments later, with a humming sound and a click, the pod had been returned to the sales assistant with your change and a receipt. While this was happening, the sales assistant would be wrapping your purchase. There were lots of shuttles whizzing around on wires above your head, and it was good fun trying to run and keep up with them. Until, of course, the inevitable happened and you bumped into someone. The assistant would then return you to your parent or guardian. If no adult was present, which was often the case, a quick exit was made with a member of staff in close pursuit ensuring that you left the premises.

The Windsor Liberal Club is housed in a modern building. It reopened in 1986 with it's main entrance now in Victoria Street. The building that previously occupied the site had quite an interesting history. In 1833 it was the home of the Infirmary. The Windsor Savings Bank occupied the adjacent building. When the Post Office took over the Savings Bank, that part of the building became vacant. The Dispensary that had been situated in Church Street since 1818 then transferred to this empty section. With these two services now being conveniently situated next to each other, another floor was added to accommodate increasing demand.

All was well for approximately sixty years until 1900 when it became evident that completely new and larger premises were required. The position and shape of the building necessitated that narrow and awkward stairs had

The gateway above is in the new Barrack building and is not used as the main entrance. This is situated in Sheet Street opposite York House. The old main gate and guardroom were in this position

to be negotiated. With the advancement of medical practises, and with more sophisticated equipment being used, the situation became impossible. After much discussion, and the necessary fund-raising activities, in 1909 the King Edward VII hospital was built and opened.

It was built on land opposite the Combimere Barracks in St Leonard's Road. It was a fine, modern building, which has been added to over the years. The land it was built on had previously been the site of another hospital called The Hospital of Blessed Peter for lepers. It had been built using a grant from King Henry II in 1168 and served the poor of the district for nearly four hundred years.

There was also a hospital in Sheet Street in 1603, the exact position of which is not known. Evidently, the people of Windsor have been well looked after for centuries.

The Windsor Liberal Club moved into the now empty Infirmary and Dispensary building from their clubhouse in Peascod Street. This was to be their home until the old building was demolished. A brand new complex

This building in Church Street was used as the Dispensary from 1818 until it moved next to the Infirmary in Victoria Street

This is the same building in Church Street today

The old Infirmary and Dispensary building in the late 1800s before
the Windsor Liberal Club used it as it's headquarters (viewed from Victoria Street)

The new complex built on the site of the old Infirmary.
The Liberal Club uses part of this building now

King Edward VII hospital opened in 1909. Built on the site of the old hospital for lepers

King Edward VII hospital undergoing renovation today

Windsor Liberal Rifle Club team about to set off for a competition at Bisley in the 1950s
From the top left: Bob Hughes (my father), Arthur Glass, not known, Laurie Higley, not known, not known, Trevor Saunders, not known

The old graveyard and Madeira Walk

was built in its place. The Windsor Liberal Rifle Club had a rifle range in the 1940s and 1950s. This was situated in the cellars of the old Infirmary building. Both my mother and father were members. When I was about 12 years old, I was allowed to do a little shooting myself.

The cellars were a spooky place. They had many small rooms with walls of glazed brick, and there was little natural light. When attending the club, I often considered what ghastly conditions the patients had to endure when operations were being performed in the early days of medicine, especially before the advent of pre-med injections and anaesthetics.

During the early post-war years, it was permissible to carry a rifle through the streets, provided that it was suitably encased. There was a strict licensing procedure for firearms; it stated that ammunition was to be kept separately from the rifle, whether at home or in transit. A police officer would visit the house annually to check on the safekeeping of the weapon and ammunition. He would then only reissue the license if he were satisfied that the law was being upheld. These regulations were soon to alter; the law was changed so that both weapons and ammunition had to be kept in a secure armoury in the rifle club itself.

The Liberal Club was to feature a lot during my childhood. On summer Sunday evenings, my parents used to like to go for a stroll. If we turned left when leaving the house in Arthur Road, it meant that it was just a stroll, but if we turned right, it usually meant a visit to the Liberal Club for a drink and a chat. Ladies were not allowed in the bar; an adjoining room was made available for them and their children. Drinks were only available from the bar and had to be brought through by the menfolk. This usually consisted of a shandy for the ladies and lemonade for the children. The children were sometimes allowed out onto the Acre to walk across to the old graveyard on the other side of Madeira Walk. Kids being kids, and the Acre being gravel and earth, our Sunday best clothes soon got very dirty. This was usually followed by a severe reprimand from our parents. As time went by, and attitudes began to change, the womenfolk were given equal rights and were able to use the main bar, provided, that is, they were accompanied by a man. This new ruling did not go down well with some of the older, more staid members, some of whom refused to accept the situation and terminated their membership.

On New Years Eve, there was always a large gathering at the club, and occasionally, a child was allowed to sit in the corner to see in the New Year. My father would slip out unnoticed at eleven O'clock. He would dress up as Old Father Tyme, and at a few minutes to midnight he would appear and give a speech about the happenings in the old year and wish everyone luck and a Happy New Year. As the clock struck midnight, he would disappear out of the bar and a young baby would be brought in to symbolise the coming

Windsor Liberal Club in the late 1940's. This photograph was taken on the Acre before departing for the coast

of the New Year. By this time the baby was usually crying, having been woken up by the peals of laughter and the singing of Auld Lang Syne.

The club annual outing to the seaside was a wet occasion (inside I mean) and was usually to one of the South Coast resorts about seventy miles away. The journey took about four and a half hours. The vehicles used were partly to blame for this long journey time. There were times, when negotiating steep hills, that the driver had to change down into first gear. Another contributing factor was that motorways were not yet in existence so many winding roads and small villages had to be negotiated. The biggest factor was the refreshment stops, usually made on a country road with a wide grass verge with enough room for a coach to park. When the luggage compartment was opened, it was amazing to see just how many crates of beer had been stashed away, especially considering that half the passengers were women and children. The funniest sight was just before leaving, when a row of heads could be seen showing above the nearest hedge. I don't suppose that the ladies had such a comfortable time, considering their disposition.

There was always a little gamble on the way to the coast. Before starting out, one arrow was marked in chalk on one rear wheel arch of the coach. The wheel was then sectioned up like a roulette wheel, with one number for each passenger. Each person then placed a stake of one old shilling, which was usually held by the driver. When the coach arrived at the coast, there was a rush to see whose number was line up with the arrow and had won the prize. The lucky person then had about 35/- to spend on their annual day out. To make a comparison with today's prices, this would only buy ¾ of a pint of beer.

Chapter Four - Changing Lifestyles

My Victorian Grandparents had a very distinctive effect on my upbringing and eventually, my outlook on life. It had shown me a glimpse of a way of life that can now only be read about. Their house in Adelaide Square was a sought after type of property, even more so these days, despite inflated property prices. From the outside, this terraced house still looks as it did in those early post-war days, but inside it now has all the trappings of modern society.

On Sundays, there were three church services to attend. Obviously, these dominated the day, with meals being served at set times. Lunch was a family affair, with my grandfather carving at the table. Later, 'High Tea', piano recitals and songs from my aunt were the entertainment for the evening. These took place in the 'front room' (the best room), which was only used on Sundays, or if a visitor should call. Grandfather Bench, as I knew him, had false teeth, and when he chewed they used to chomp. It was considered bad manners to talk at the table, except for polite conversation such as "pass the salt please", so the chomping noise was quite noticeable, but of course, nothing was said. Aunt Edie, a prim and proper lady, was more like a housekeeper in this Victorian run household. Being my grandfather's second wife, she was never really accepted by the children. As I grew older, I realised that there had been a deep resentment towards their second mother, and even though it had been many years since her death, their natural mother was still very dearly missed.

When the whole family gathered together at Christmas, the highlight of the evening was a game of rummy. The stakes were either tiddlywink counters or buttons from the button box (every household had one). It was quite a jolly occasion and there were usually sixteen of the family gathered together.

When both of my grandparents had passed away, and the house was being cleared, I was amazed at the neat and precise way in which everything was stored. Table cloths, and napkins with tissue paper between each one had been neatly ironed and folded in much the same way as they had been when first purchased. Each item had it's specific place in drawers and cupboards. The highly polished cutlery was still kept in its original canteen, and the crystal glasses sparkled like gems in the sunlight. Even personal items, such as underclothes, handkerchiefs and gloves had their own set places.

I was taken to the house when my grandfather died by my own Father, who was organising all the necessary arrangements. The first thing that he did when we entered the house was to make for the parlour and go over to the cupboard next to the chair where my grandfather always sat. He brought

The late Victorian terraced house in Adelaide Square

out the bottle of pure malt whiskey (kept for purely medicinal purposes) . He then took a good long swig form the bottle, turned to me, and said "Well, he won't mind now, will he?'

The most vivid memory I have of the house in Adelaide Square was of the outside toilet at the bottom of the garden, with it's candle, matches and newspaper squares hung on a string. I never did know whether the newspaper was used out of meanness, or whether toilet paper was difficult to obtain during the post-war years.

It was a harsh winter in 1947 and the rivers were running very high. There had been a heavy snowfall, followed by a quick thaw. Together, these caused one of the worst floods Windsor has ever known. It was a Sunday morning, and I had been playing with Meccano sets one and two that I had been given for Christmas and my birthday which followed soon after. Lunch had been prepared, but by now, everyone was standing at the front door staring with amazement at the water coming around Vatise's corner and into Arthur Road from Goswell Road. At first, the drains coped, but soon the road was covered. The terraced housed in Arthur Road on the side of the Noah's Ark pub (a name soon to become very appropriate), had one step down into the hallway. The sandbags that had been previously issued for such an occasion proved

Grandfather Bench, Constable No. 17 in 1909.
A visitor to Windsor sent this photograph to him

to be useless. Already the flooding was quite extensive in Oxford Road and around the 'Low Level' (the local name for the road that ran from the Noah's Ark to Barry Avenue). Soon, the whole area became flooded, and within a couple of days the situation began to look quite serious. The water level began to rise and was now mixed with drain water.

The house that we lived in was on the opposite side to the Noah's Ark. These properties had five steps leading up to the front doors. After five or six days, the water was still rising and everyone was living upstairs. There was no fresh water, electricity or gas by this time. With three or four feet of water in the house, the situation necessitated that all the services had been switched off. From the fourth night onwards, a night watchman rowed up and p?wn the flooded roads so that he could be available to anyone with an

Arthur Road in the early days of the floods, before the families started to evacuate

View of the Gasworks yard during the 1947 floods looking down Goswell Lane from the Railway Viaduct

emergency. The noise of the oars in the rollicks, and the splash of the oars as thy entered the water was a comfort during the otherwise deathly silence of the pitch-black nights. In those flooded areas of Windsor, a few deliveries, such as bread and milk, were made by punt. Items were handed up to bedroom windows in a basket attached to a pole. A few of the men had fishermen's waders and were at first able to walk through the floodwater, but it soon became so deep that even this was impossible. By now any item that was not secured was floating around.

There were also dead livestock and the occasional pet cat or dog that had perished. By this time, the water contained sewerage as well. The Ayres family occupied the house opposite. They had managed to save their chickens and were good enough to share their eggs with us. This was made possible by a makeshift 'Breeches Buoy' being set up. For a while we were able to exchange goods that each family was short of, but eventually the line snapped. By now, the situation was becoming impossible and families were being evacuated daily. This was a tricky job; the best way was to climb out of the bedroom window and down a ladder to the Army DUKWs (amphibious vehicles). The alternative was to have a piggyback from half way up the stairs from a volunteer. This was a little dangerous as the water had moved around loose items and it was very easy to trip over them. Getting your legs and bottom wet was one thing, but a complete drenching is another. The DUKWs then took the evacuees to a sloping road called Sydney Place. This enabled the passengers to disembark and walk through Creeks Cut into Peascod Street.

We stayed with relatives in Nelson Road at Clewer, not very far from the Convent of St John the Baptist in Hatch Lane. Clewer was still very rural. Some of the land belonged to the Convent and some was still being farmed by local landowners, although it was gradually being sold off for housing development. I was fascinated by the fact that milk was delivered in the evening straight form the farm in handheld churns, immediately after he milking was complete.

The sounds of the country were so different from those of the Gasworks and goods yard, but after a few days it was heaven, and very enjoyable. Alas, all had to change again. After about two weeks, when the floodwaters had receded, it was time to move back. Usually, it was the menfolk first; there was an awful mess and a lot of bad smells. As the water had receded, it had left behind waves of mud and slime, up to a foot deep inside the houses. Most of the furniture and belongings were useless after being in the dirty water for such a long time.

When the initial cleanup was well advanced, it was time for the womenfolk and children to return. Ventilation of the houses was the first priority. Doors and windows were left open as much as possible. Airbricks were removed, and floorboards in each of the downstairs rooms were lifted to enhance the airflow. For a long time after the flood, it was damp, smelly and musty in the house. It was months, rather than weeks that the floorboards were left up for. When eventually they were put back, and new linoleum laid, mould would appear occasionally on the floors and walls.

During 1948, a family who lived in the new prefabricated homes at Hill Top Road (now known as Camm Avenue) hated it so much at Dedworth that they desperately wanted to move back into the town centre again. The exchange was arranged, despite the 'Prefabs', as they were known, being ultra-modern, and the houses near the gasworks still being damp. The dislike of this new estate was so great for the family that the exchange was completed.

Prior to the floods, large lorries had been seen passing through Windsor with prefabricated sections of houses secured on the back. It was later discovered that each had comprised of nearly a quarter of a new home. This was a new concept in housing and was quite often the butt of a joke. At the time, I never imagined that one day I would be living in one of those flimsy looking homes. As it happens, these were magnificent homes, and although the original concept was for a five to ten year life span, they were not actually pulled down until the mid-seventies when the whole area was redeveloped. As for the prefabs themselves, they turned out to be an insight into how the modern home of today looks. Each one was completely surrounded by garden. Inside there were plenty of built-in cupboards. The kitchen had a refrigerator built in under the worktop, which stretched from wall to wall. There was also a boiler and wringer strategically placed next to the sink. This had a lift-up worktop for convenient use on washdays. The toilet was separate from the bathroom which, in the forties, was a feature normally only found in quite expensive homes. It was quite a contrast to the old terraced houses of Arthur Road with their outside conveniences and no bathrooms.

The Convent of St John the Baptist has played a big part in the history of Windsor. It was founded in 1852 and has always been a 'Mother House'. John Armstrong, the one time Bishop of Grahamstown had advocated that the work at the Convent should be by the ladies of higher classes (Sisters of Mercy) and should help the poor and needy. The cholera outbreak of 1849 contributed to the notorious conditions in the slums of Bier Street, now River Street. The old buildings stood where the River Street car park is now situated. Another slum, even more notorious, was situated at Clewer Fields, which is in between Oxford Road and Bexley Street. The Bier Street site housed 259 people in 33 dwellings while Clewer Fields housed 291 people in 69 dwellings. Not many of these were privately owned, but were lodging houses or beer houses. There were also many brothels.

Bier Lane (River Street) in the mid 1800s – this was pulled down and made into a car park. It used to be known as the Italienne Quarter

A view after the Italienne Quarter was demolished in River Street

River Street car park as it is today

Clewer Houses of Mercy Laundry in the early years

The Sister's Garden

Haymaking in the 30s

There are two barracks in Windsor, which in the early days billeted a thousand men between them. The town at this time also had an influx of navvies who had been brought in to work on the two rival railways being built. The slums are reputed to have been the worst outside of London. The Convent, in it's early days, built up a large workforce, and gave the poor girls who were caught up in this distasteful way of life an education and a home. In many cases it gave them back their self-respect.

Chapter Five - Dideorde Manor

The Doomsday Manor of Dideorde in the Hundreds of Ripplesmore gave its name to an area of Windsor now known as Dedworth. It was such an exciting place for a nine-year-old to live and play, with an abundance of countryside and lots of new places to explore. I continued to attend the Royal Free Junior School until I was old enough to sit the 'eleven plus' examinations. This was a most decisive time at school and determined whether you were bound for Grammar or Secondary School. To me, the most outstanding feature of this school was the purpose built gymnasium which, because of its size, doubled up for a theatre for school plays using a portable stage at one end. Looking back, I recall that the building was old, but extremely well maintained. It had winding stone staircases with glazed brick walls and highly polished floors. Outside, the iron staircases were painted black. Purely by chance, and just before the building ceased to be used as a school in 1987 (thirty-seven years after attending the school myself), the then Headmistress decided that an open evening for former pupils was to be held. Those who wished to do so could return to see the buildings again and possibly rekindle childhood memories. I took this opportunity and found that my memories had not been those seen through rose-tinted spectacles. Much to my delight, it was just as I had remembered. The school building then stood empty for many years and started to become derelict. Eventually it was converted and furnished and is now let out as private dwellings. From the outside it looks very much as it did all those years ago, but without the toilet blocks or gymnasium. These have been demolished and replaced by a purpose built modern library. The house where the Headmaster used to live still stands next to the old school building and is also now a private dwelling.

When attending Royal Free Junior School, and while still living in Arthur Road, I was able to go home sometimes during the lunch hour. One day my best friend came home with me. When we were walking back to school and passing through Sydney Place one hot summers day, I asked him if he got sunburned very much, referring to his dark brown arms. There was a pause and he gave me a stern look and said 'Yer tryin' t'be funny mate?' in a strong West African accent. Try to imagine calling someone 'Sambo' these days, even your best mate. There was no offence meant, and none taken. After all, such names as 'Curly', 'Ginger' and 'Shorty' were widely used. During the two years that I knew him, I never did find out his surname. I was always 'Stew' to him and he was always 'Sambo' to me.

How I envied those boys who were transported to and from school by bus from the big house in the country at Winkfield. But how could I have

The old Royal Free School building on the Acre is now six private dwellings

been so naïve? Nice as New Lodge, the Dr Barnardo's home was, my parents were there to look after me when I got home from school, and I did not have to sleep in a dormitory with nine other boys.

When the time came to sit the eleven plus, naturally everyone hoped they would do well. Those who failed would return to the senior part of the school in the same building, and did so with trepidation. The Headmaster, a Mr Sykes, had an awesome reputation as a strict disciplinarian and was not shy of using the cane. Many a boy already attending this school lived in fear of crossing this man, and those about to enter were told stories by their friends or brothers who had first hand experience. I never became a 'Big Boy' as they were called at this school, as I failed the eleven plus. As I now lived in Dedworth, I was allocated a place at the Clarence Road Secondary Modern School (now known as Trevelyan) which was half the distance to travel from my new home at Hill Top Road. Needless to say, I never did find out first hand if Mr Sykes was as bad as he was made out to be.

The Headmaster at the new school was a Mr Cawsey. He was a strict but fair man. I remember he had a shiny, balding head. Each morning, the school song was sung at Assembly, accompanied by Miss Smith on the piano. It consisted of two verses taken from the Harrow School Song and was called Forty Years On. The Lords Prayer and any other business of the day followed this. The two verses that were sung are as follows:

New Lodge at Winkfield in the late 40s and 50s, when the house was used as a Dr Barnardo's home

Verse 1

Forty years on when afar and asunder
Parting are those who are singing today
When you look back and forget fully wonder
What you were like in your work and your play
Then it may be, there will come o'er you
Glimpses of notes like the catch of a song
Visions of boyhood shall float them before you
Echoes of dreamland shall bear them along
Follow up, follow up, follow up, follow up, follow up, follow up,
Till the field ring again and again
With the tramp of twenty-two men
Follow up, follow up.

Verse 4

Forty years on growing older and older
Shorter in wind as in memory long
Feeble on foot and rheumatic of shoulder
What will it help you that once you were strong
God gave us bases to guard out beleaguer
Games to play out, whether earnest of fun
Fights for the fearless and goals for the eager
Twenty and thirty and forty years on
Follow up

The two teachers that I remember most vividly during my senior school days were firstly Mr Monk. He taught physical education and mathematics. I always liked his method of teaching as he made lessons fun. During a maths lesson, he would often include a small general knowledge quiz incorporating geography and maths together. I feel that if I had been taught the subject all the time by this teacher, I would have taken more of an interest in the subject, but alas, the maths teacher changed. Soon after this, the school introduced basic decimals. It was at this stage that I became hopelessly lost and never really caught up. During one of Mr Monk's quizzes, he asked where on the map of England you would send your dirty laundry. My hand shot up immediately and I answered 'The Wash Sir'. From that day forwards, I never forgot the location of that area on the map. To this day, I firmly believe that if learning can be made fun from an early age, information is so much easier to retain.
    The last session of P.E. in the term was usually made into a triple period. This enabled the gymnasium to be set up for a game called British Bulldog. It entailed using all the equipment at once, including the wall bars and ropes, and took quite a long time to set up. The class was divided into two teams; the attackers and the defenders. The aim of the defenders was to prevent the attackers from reaching the other end of the hall without their feet touching the floor. The defenders were allowed to take one step in only one direction from their original position. Each attacking team member received one point if he managed to get through and shout 'British Bulldog, One, Two, Three' upon arrival at the opposite end. When the first team had completed the course, the roles were reversed. The winners were the team with the most points. This game was very rough and exciting, although very enjoyable.
    The other teacher I remember well was a Miss Smith. She taught French to both sexes and Needlework to the girls. Very soon after I started taking French lessons, the subject was discontinued as a compulsory subject at the school.
    Miss Smith was a name on everyone's lips at the school. She was a very staid type of person who rarely smiled and wore thick makeup and strong perfume. She was a strict disciplinarian but was respected by everyone. I revisited the school a couple of years after leaving. By this time I was living in London while serving my apprenticeship. After visiting the Headmaster and a couple of other teachers who were enjoying a free period in the staff room, I made my way out of the school. While passing the block of new classrooms which had low windows allowing a view right inside the classroom, I found myself (I don't know why) knocking on Miss Smith's classroom door while a needlework lesson was in progress. Upon entering, there was a deathly silence and that familiar smell of perfume. After a small amount of tittering and a stern 'Quiet please, work on your own for a little

The Copper Horse, the equestrian statue of King George III at the top of Snow Hill, 3 miles from Windsor Castle

while' from Miss Smith, we had a short chat and shook hands on parting. Subsequently, whenever our paths crossed around town, we always stopped and exchanged a few pleasantries. It was on occasions like this that I realised that Miss Smith was really quite a nice person. Many years later this was borne out by an obituary to her in the local paper. I was quite amazed at the glowing words written about her.

To this day, I don't really know what made me go into a class of forty giggling girls to speak to her.

I used to look forward to games periods and loved cross-country running. Windsor Great Park was the usual venue for this activity with the route being via Stag meadow (the home of the Windsor and Eton Football Club) to the Copper Horse on Snow Hill and back. This fitted quite nicely into the allotted double period. It was also the last period of the day, so if there was any hold up, it did not disrupt any other lessons.

Aboard the Royal Daffodil with my parents

I was also a member of the drama group and usually got a non-speaking part in the Christmas school plays. Emil and the Detectives was one of the favourites. Alice, Thomas and Jane was another. In the latter, I was given the part of the bear, mainly because of my size. It was very hot inside that bearskin, and I spent many hours perfecting authentic bear movements.

During the summer holidays, the school organised trips to the Lake District. These were only available to those in the 'A' stream. Unfortunately, I only managed to get as high as the 'B' stream throughout my schooling, but this did not stop me from wanting to join in. Even if I had been eligible to go, my parents would have found it very difficult financially. On the day of departure, I would cycle down to the school and wave goodbye. I then cycled back home with sadness and disappointment in my heart. I was also annoyed at myself for not getting into the higher grade, but even if I had managed this, financially I wouldn't have been in with a chance.

The very first year at senior school, my parents did manage to save up for a week's holiday. It was to be their first since the war. It took them a whole year to gather the money together, but they managed it. It was to be a holiday that I have never forgotten. It started with a train journey to London from Windsor and Eton Riverside station. Usually, holiday journeys were by

Windsor and Eton Riverside Station

train or coach, but on arrival at Waterloo station, instead of changing trains, the journey was completed by boat from the Tower Pier to Margate Pier. These trips could either be taken on a day, or period return basis. Those old paddle steamers were a delightfully relaxing way to travel. A day trip started at 8am and arrived at 12:30pm, allowing three and a half hours at the seaside before leaving at 4pm for the return journey. The name of the boat that we travelled on was the Royal Daffodil. Other boats on the river were Royal Eagle and Golden Eagle. There was one more boat that used to be in the same fleet, but unfortunately this had been lost at the Dunkirk evacuation a few years earlier. The adult period return fare was 10/6d (52 $^{1}/_{2}$ p).

When we first moved to Dedworth, I was able to earn extra pocket money from my father. The wheelbarrow that had been purpose-built for collecting coke from the Gasworks came into its own when creating a new garden. The Prefabs had ample ground at the front and rear. My father was in his element and soon found that the allotment he rented while living in Arthur Road was no longer necessary. He was far too busy creating flowerbeds and a vegetable plot from the then virgin farmland at Hill Top. This estate was built on a north facing hillside and enjoyed panoramic views across the Thames Valley to Cliveden and beyond.

The soil was clay and required a lot of breaking down. I was paid an old threepenny piece for each barrow of leaf mould that I brought back from the adjoining forest. This was a task I undertook frequently in the first year. When it came time for the holiday in Margate, I had some extra money to spend. It felt all the better knowing all the hard work that had gone into earning it. As always, I was shown a good example and encouraged to spend only a third and save the remainder.

Another task on arrival at Hill Top was to make coal briquettes from the dust in the coal bunker. This was achieved using a light mixture of cement and coal dust, which was poured, into the moulds. When the mixture was set, they were turned out and the process repeated until all of the coal dust had been used up. The briquettes helped to eke out the coal supply for a while during the winter months. This was quite a help financially as 1 hundredweight of coal cost 15/- (old shillings).

My childhood leaves me with many good memories, but there are always bad ones as well. I can't remember having any dental check-ups at junior school, but they were the order of the day when attending Clarence Road Secondary Modern. What caused my extreme fear of the annual dentist visit I do not know, but it was very real. The fear started when the word got around that the dentist was in the area. I used to get all churned up inside just a the thought of a check-up, and became even worse if it was found that I needed treatment. The dental records were kept in alphabetical order. As the time for my visit got nearer, I wished that my surname began with the letter z. Of course, with hindsight, it would only have prolonged the agony. I remember, as it got nearer to my turn, and a date was given, I used to feel quite unwell, and sometimes developed a temperature. When the dreaded day arrived, I always seemed to need to have some teeth removed. The exact procedure is as clear in my mind today as it was real at the time.

The surgery was a large building in it's own grounds at the corner of Hatch Lane, opposite the Three Elms public house. The waiting room was a stark, bare room with only a few chairs around the edge, and smelled of antiseptic. When your turn came, whoever was accompanying you (mostly mothers in those days) stayed in the waiting room while you went through a door at the other end of the room. This led into an anteroom with linoleum on the floor and no furniture. The smell of antiseptic was even stronger now. Your footsteps echoed as you walked across the room to another door opposite that led straight into the surgery itself. By this time, fear had blanked out any details except for the experience of sitting in the chair with a rubber tasting plug holding my mouth open and a rubber mask being held firmly over my nose. The taste of the plug together with the smell of the gas and the claustrophobic effect of the mask, combined with the buzzing noise in the head as the anaesthetic took effect was horrendous. I used to struggle, but was restrained by firm hands. Suddenly, it was all over. The discomfort of the extraction was a pleasant release from the mental and emotional torture that had been going on inside me for weeks. The (almost) pleasurable experience of the intravenous injection used by modern surgery today is a far cry from the nightmare visits to the school dentist.

The Windsor Liberal Club features quite frequently in my early years. By now, the club had quite a substantial female membership, which was increasing all the time. The members put on an annual concert in the hall above the rifle range. I believe it was called the Victoria Hall. When looking back, it amazes me the amount of hidden talent that could be found amongst its members. I liken it to an amateur version of Opportunity Knocks, but without the competitive element. There was one lady in particular, a Mrs Greenwood, the manageress of Freeman, Hardy and Willis, the shoe shop in Peascod Street. She had a marvellous soprano voice. During one of her acts, she sang the song 'I'm the biggest aspidistra in the world'. Prior to the start of the show, and with her permission, two artificial aspidistra plants were placed in mock up flowerpots on the stage in front of the proscenium arch. Attached to each plant was a fine white thread. During the song, a stagehand would pull the plants up very slowly as if they were growing. Usually, they were halfway up the proscenium arch before anyone would notice. Tittering would then start, and perhaps someone would point. The tittering would become whispers accompanied by fidgeting and then the hall would return to silence while the performance was completed. Rather tame by today's special effects, but very effective at the time.

Chapter Six – The Teenage Years

After an evening at the club, my parents would often walk the two miles home to Dedworth. On one particular occasion, it was rather late and the last bus had left long ago. It was a fine, but crisp and cold night and we were accompanied by a Mr and Mrs Harris. While walking along Clarence Road, approaching the junction with Imperial Road (the roundabout, Goslar Way and the relief road had not yet been built), a vehicle approached at great speed along Imperial road and turned right almost on two wheels. It missed us by only a few feet. It then zigzagged, clipping hedges and garden walls and sped off towards Windsor. The driver was later apprehended in Slough. The term 'Drink Driving' had not become fashionable at the time, but even on the comparatively empty roads of the early 1950s, it was obviously a menace. Needless to say, the incident was a shock to us all, but especially Mr Harris who had never driven or owned a car. He had recently retired and purchased a bungalow in St Andrew's Crescent after a lifetime working as a Master Tailor in London. This journey he had made twice a day for the past thirty years, catching the train from the Windsor and Eton Riverside Station to London Waterloo. His position had necessitated that he wear a pin-striped suit and bowler hat while carrying an umbrella and briefcase. The journey time of nearly fifty minutes was roughly the same as it is today, and he would have been quite comfortable sitting in the First Class compartment reading his copy of the Times newspaper which he had previously purchased from W.H.Smiths kiosk on the station forecourt. Quite a difference from today's journeys, with tourists, backpackers, cycles and unruly youngsters, often eating, drinking and swearing, and all crammed into the one compartment carriages while trying not to listen to other people's mobile phone conversations.

On another occasion, a hot summers night, Mrs Harris and my mother were walking in front busily chatting away (as ladies do), when my father dashed across the road into the Three Elms public house, downed a double, and was back behind the ladies before either of them realised what had happened!

My father always liked a tipple, sometimes too frequently. My mother liked to keep him in check but was not always successful.

Shortly after moving to Dedworth, I was enrolled at a Sunday School. I hated this part of the week. I was made to dress up in my 'Sunday Best', peaked cap and all, and told to attend. I really did not like it and many times I skived off. I took to walking the streets for the allotted time and then returning home as if all was well. This worked fine until one day a neighbour commented to my mother that I looked smart on Sunday when she saw me

The Three Elms Public House

on Park Corner. The only trouble was that Park Corner was in the opposite direction to the Sunday School meeting. The cat was out of the bag and I was in big trouble. After a long period, my parents saw reason, and I was allowed to join the Sea Cadets. I was never forced to go to Sunday School again.

The Windsor Sea Cadets is the founder unit of the movement. In 1899, Queen Victoria made a £10 donation. Eton College and the local council of the time made further contributions. Together with money that was raised from various events, this was used to purchase a Dutch Barge, which was used as their headquarters. This was moored at Thamesside, outside the Donkey House, a drinking hostelry by the river. When it was formed, the organisation was named the Navy Lads Brigade. It then became the Navy League Lads and finally the Sea Cadets Association, the name by which it is known today. The idea behind the organisation was to try and recruit

Windsor Sea Cadets circa 1905

youngsters and encourage them towards a life at sea. In the late 1800s, the Army had a recruiting system and the Navy was finding it difficult to find able bodied young men who were interested in sailing the world in a Man-O-War, so the movement was born.

On Sunday mornings there was often a church parade. The chosen squad formed outside their headquarters in Barry Avenue and marched through the town in full ceremonial dress. This consisted of white gloves, hat and belt and gaiters with a .22 ceremonial rifle. Following the church service in the Parish Church in the High Street, and after returning to headquarters, those who wished, changed into jumpers. They then partook in a trip in the unit's twenty-seven foot whaler – quite a handful for a group of eleven and twelve-year olds. On one particular occasion, the CO had misjudged the strength of the midwinter current and we were nearly carried under the road bridge at Jennings Wharf and into the weir stream. It was only the excellent training and the discipline that had been instilled into us that prevented the Sunday outing becoming a tragedy.

I was continuously in trouble with my parents because these outings often lasted until 2pm and Sunday lunch was served at 1pm with no exceptions. I was often late and got into heaps of trouble over this as I was torn between two loyalties.

During the two years that I was a cadet, a week's holiday was arranged aboard an old destroyer called HMS Dido. She was anchored permanently in Portsmouth Harbour and was used as a training ship. It was the first time that I had stayed away from home, but I had a smashing week and had many stories to tell my friends at school when the summer holidays were over.

I will always remember sleeping in a hammock. When the time came to sling your hammock up, if you were not quick enough to find a decent place,

Aboard HMS Dido circa 1953
The boy on the left was my partner in the washing up crime.
Ken Crummack in the centre was my best mate at school.
I am the boy on the right.

you took what was left. The only place I could find was across an open hatch, which led down to the engine room far below. It was a good job that I had learned to tie my knots properly! We went rowing in a 30ft cutter on the sea and were amazed at the size of the wake from an ocean-going liner passing about two miles away.

I never liked washing up, and when it was my turn, the boy who shared the arduous task with me also felt the same way. We decided that the best way to solve the problem was to drop the dirty plates and cutlery out of the nearest porthole and into the harbour. So that was exactly what we did. Fortunately for the Navy, we were only there for a week.

Many hours of my time when we first moved to Dedworth was spent playing in the forest adjoining the estate at Hill Top Road. This land was totally unspoilt and sloped quite steeply in places down from an old track called the Red Road. The name speaks for itself, as the earth beneath the gravel was quite red. On the other side of the road, the land was fenced off and clearly marked 'Private'. This formed part of the St Leonard's Hill estate. Deep inside the estate, on the crest of a hill, was the ruin of an old house known locally as Barries Ruins. It could be a dangerous place because of the

Group in front of a float made for a Windsor Carnival procession

loose stonework and unsteady columns. Some of the ground floor rooms still maintained quite extensive mosaic floors, although the fauna over the year had overgrown most of it. Enough was left uncovered though, and with a little imagination, a picture emerged of the magnificence of the old house in it's prime. The extensive cellars below were ideal for playing hide and seek, although in some places brickwork and earth had fallen in. Of course, as kids, we had no fear of the dangers of playing in such a place, especially as it was so isolated. A few times when heading for the ruins, we were caught by the gamekeeper and sent packing with a flea in our ear. I suppose that the keen ear of an experienced man with a good sense of direction could hear the noise we made while clambering through the undergrowth on the way to the ruins.

The hours spent playing in the forest below the Red Road were fun. Most of the places were given names such as 'The Hollow Tree', 'The Old Oak', 'The Bridge', 'The Ups and Downs' and 'The Thicket'. We used to make bows and arrows. The arrows had to be carefully chosen from young saplings and were given a pointed tip. We used to make low hiding places in the bracken, carefully replacing the top layer and making detection almost impossible. In the winter, we would dam the fast flowing streams and when the spring arrived, we would trespass onto farmland, being careful not to get caught. This was accomplished by using the cover of hedgerows and thickets. The object of the outings was to reach a place about a mile away that we called the 'Second Forest'. It was here that bluebells grew in abundance. They grew so tall and close together that it was just like a carpet. We picked armfuls to take home to our mothers. On the way, we lost quite a few, and by the journey's end, the rest were beginning to droop; the only way to carry them was over two outstretched arms held against our bodies. Of course, our mothers didn't know that we had been trespassing. Well, I don't think so anyway.

At the bottom of our garden was a runner bean frame and behind which was a compost heap. After the conker season had finished, any leftovers were dumped on the compost. After a few years, along the bottom of the garden, a few saplings started to grow.

By the time I left school, and subsequently left home at sixteen to work in London, a couple of the saplings had reached a height of 5-6 feet. Several years later, when the prefabs were pulled down for redevelopment, one of the trees was left as part of the landscape. Nearly fifty years later, it is a fine specimen of a horse chestnut tree. Whenever I pass by, it brings back fond memories of the carefree childhood days at Dedworth.

While researching this book, I drove along the Red Road, now known as St Leonard's Hill. The land on both sides has now been extensively developed and is hardly recognisable. One of the few very large houses that had access from the Red Road in the old days was one called Byways. It belonged to the owner of Windsorian Coaches. I could not find this house, but in it's place was a cul-de-sac called Coombes Hill Court, which in itself supports half a dozen magnificent houses.

I used to go with a friend and his elder brother to do odd jobs in the grounds of Byways, cleaning up mainly. The oldest boy was given the much sought after job of sitting astride the very large petrol driven mower and cutting the grass of the extensive lawns. Alan, his brother and I had the never-ending job of removing the long, thin, stubborn stems of grass that the mower had pushed over instead of cutting off. The only real way of seeing these was to get on our hands and knees with our heads down, looking along the lawn, and pulling them out by hand. As I recall, there was no reward for this task, but copious amounts of ice cold home made lemonade, served in a tall glass jug with a plate of fancy biscuits. This was brought out by one of the house staff on a silver tray. Needless to say this was very welcome in the hot summer days of yesteryear.

The most regular job that I had as a boy was working for Penicud's Dairy. In the first instance, I did the round with Mr Penicud himself. The dairy was situated in St Leonard's Road in a property that backed onto the cemetery. Some of the smaller, independent dairies had been taken over by larger ones such as the Windsor and Eton Dairies, which in turn had been taken over by the large conglomerates. Nowadays, with milk being sold in so many outlets, the milk roundsman is fast disappearing altogether. It was fun working on Saturdays and during the school holidays with the same milkman on the same round. It was a well spread out round covering quite a distance. On Saturday, which was money-collecting day, I started at 6:30 am. Jack, the roundsman was already loaded up and ready to start when I arrived. The day normally ended about two or three o'clock when I usually unloaded while Jack cashed up. Being such a long day, I took along sandwiches and cake, but there was never any shortage of drinks of orange or tea, especially once I became known and was a regular helper.

Throughout the year, I made some tips, and usually ended up with about 7s6d on a Saturday morning (equivalent to 35 $^{1}/_{2}$p now). As I grew older, I even had my own money satchel and completed transactions on my own. The last Christmas that I worked at the dairy, my tips amounted to £17. The average weekly wage for tradesman then was about £10-10s. Needless to say, I was very well pleased.

One major incident that happened while I was working at the dairy was on a Saturday. The driveway to the yard was quite wide. Along one wall were stacked all the stray milk bottles that had found their way back to the depot. They were on their sides with their bottoms against the wall. This wall of bottles grew larger throughout the year, and was held in place by large concrete blocks at each end. Every so often, when enough bottles had been collected, they were sorted and returned to the relevant dairies in the district. On one particular occasion, when a sort out was well overdue, the milk transporter delivering the next day's milk supply clipped one of the concrete blocks and moved it. With a deafening sound, thousands of bottles smashed to smithereens all over the driveway. This mess took a couple of hours to clear up. As each milk float returned to the dairy, the roundsman would help with the clear up. When this had been done, the transporter was then able to reverse out of the yard. The milk floats that were parked in the road outside the dairy shop were then driven in, unloaded and plugged into the charger ready for the next day's deliveries.

After working with the dairy for a few years, I took a job with Reeves the butchers which was situated on the corner of River Street, opposite the Castle. As was to be expected for a youngster, I was given all the 'good jobs', as they were called. One in particular used to be completed every other Saturday. This was the emptying of the brine tub situated at the back of the walk-in fridge and filling it with a new brine mixture. The cutting room for the shop and the walk-in fridge were below the shop floor. The only access was by ladder through a trapdoor in the corner of the shop. On delivery days, all carcasses were lowered by pulley into the cutting room. It was always very cold down there, and with no natural light, it was a world of its own.

The butchers always wore mittens and the kettle was constantly on the boil. Those mugs of tea always tasted special. The best part of the day was making the deliveries around the town and into the Castle. I rode one of those old style delivery bicycles with a huge wicker basket on the front. The last part of the round was always the Castle, so the best part was being able to freewheel all the way back to the shop at the bottom of Castle Hill. The manager of the shop wanted me to work full-time when I left school, but I had my sights set on joining the Police Force. The only problem was that I had left school at the age of fifteen and a quarter, and the joining age for the Berkshire Constabulary was sixteen and a half. The school employment officer used to visit each school a few months before the end of the school year and help with placing school leavers in employment. It was normal to attend the interview with a parent, usually the mother, as the fathers were busy at work and taking time off was a much frowned upon practice. When my situation was explained to the officer, he asked me what my hobbies were. I replied that I liked cooking. He immediately picked up on this and informed me shortly afterwards that the Olde House Hotel (now the Sir Christopher Wren's House Hotel) were looking for a trainee. Both my parents were apprehensive about the situation, but agreed that I should start, as I seemed so keen. As a trainee cook, the conditions were poor and the pay even worse, although these have improved somewhat during the past forty-five years. The unsociable hours still cause havoc with family life.

During the last six months at school, I took a paper round. Shortly after starting this job, the manager of the shop changed. The new man soon had his favourites. One of the other boys had a sister who wanted a job at the shop. The new manager kept insisting that I had made up the round incorrectly, and informed me several times that I had made delivery mistakes and some customers had been complaining. He eventually sacked me. When my classmates got to hear of this, I got a lot of jibes because I had lost my job so soon. I asked the manager what houses had been complaining. When two or three were mentioned, I visited them to apologise. They did not know what I was talking about and said that all their deliveries had been correct. The very next day I went to the shop manager to complain. The manager replied that my services were no longer required and that my job had been given to somebody else and that was the end of the matter; a far cry from the procedures available to the workforce of today. This was just a glimpse of what the grown-ups' world could be like.

Chapter Seven - A Walk Through Town

During the immediate post-war years, many items were still rationed. This situation was to continue for quite some while. The war had not only taken a terrible toll on human life, but had put an immense strain on the county's resources. Now, Great Britain was heavily in debt, and had started to use its gold reserves to buy imports.

During 1947, electricity and gas had been nationalised, and on January 1948 the individual railway companies were amalgamated to become British Railways. The now infamous ship Empire Windrush had brought the first group of immigrants into Britain. As manpower was short, it was hoped that this would go part of the way to redressing the balance. If Britain was to be a world leader in the second half of the twentieth century, just as it had been for the previous hundred years, it had to be rebuilt and it's people put back to work doing what they were best at; exporting fine products to a needy world.

The men and women who were no longer required in the three Services were demobbed and given a suit to wear. These were very austere outfits, and not very popular, but it was a start for those who arrived back to dear old Blighty to find that they had lost everything, and sometimes everyone. It was a lifeline, and with a few bob in their pocket, it was a chance to start a new life in peacetime Britain.

In many families, especially among children, hand-me-downs were commonplace. Also, home made clothes for the children, when material became available, were the order of the day. The darning of socks to extend their life was also common practice. A good seamstress could alter clothes from one style to another, or to fit a younger brother or sister. It was a skill that was well sought after. It was to be quite a few years before the materials and colours that we take for granted today became available to the general public at affordable prices. The practice of changing from longjohns and thick vests to summer underwear was still common, but as new modern materials became available, this practice became less popular. It was almost twenty years before this practice died out in my parent's house.

Many families relied on the dividends (divvies) earned from shops such as the Co-Op to buy some of the basics in life. 'Club Shops', as they were called, were also very popular. Even 'Uncles' (the pawnbrokers) was frequently in use in many areas. Some women took to working part time, but this practice was frowned upon for many years. I had said to me many times 'Oh, your mother goes out to *work*, does she?'

Some women who had worked long hours in factories towards the war effort found that a little independence was a good thing and that they looked

Athens

The inscription on the memorial stone reads as follows:

'The bathing place of Athens was presented to Eton College by Hiatt C Baker in memory of his son John Lionel Baker, a brilliant swimmer who spent here many of the happiest days of his boyhood. He was killed in a flying accident in August 1917 while still a member of the school'

to escape from the drudgeries of housework and nappy changing. Some, on the other hand, had no choice, and were forced into the situation, as the breadwinner was no longer around to provide for them.

Those who were fortunate enough to have two wages coming in found that their standards improved, and perhaps instead of just one or two days at the seaside each year, they could afford a week at a boarding house.

Very shortly after moving to Dedworth, my mother, her Sister Madge, my Cousins and I used to spend days during the long summer having picnics on the Brocas, at the Eton College bathing point called Athens. One day, after walking back to Windsor, and after my aunt and Cousins had headed back to Slough, my mother took me into the ABC (Aerated Bread Co.)

Here is River Street (Bier Lane)

refreshment rooms for a cup of tea and a sticky bun. This was in the building now occupied by McDonald's. Boys being the fidget that they are, I was messing around at the table. Beneath the tabletop was a shelf for umbrellas, gloves and scarves. It was quite deep, reaching almost halfway under the table. Right at the back on my side I pulled out a package that someone had left behind. It was an envelope held closed by an elastic band. Without opening it completely, a wad of banknotes could be seen inside. My mother insisted that we made the long walk to the Police Station in St Leonard's Road to hand it in. When checked, it contained a total of £300 in £1 and £5 notes, a small fortune to a family whose total annual income was approximately £650. We never did find out if it had been claimed, or if a reward had been given. In fact, the incident only came to mind while researching this book.

The mind is such a strange thing. How could an event of this nature be forgotten for nearly fifty years? It is where this restaurant was situated that 'A Walk Through Town' begins.

The premises next door to the ABC are no15/16b Thames Street, now a Beefeater restaurant. Previously Boots the Chemist occupied this building,

A disused entrance to the Castle known as the Hundred Steps

with a lending library using the first floor. There is a flight of stone steps next to this building which lead to the public gardens below. These are known as Boots Steps. Sir Jesse Boot gave this land to the townspeople of Windsor. The steps were opened by the Countess of Athlone in 1921.

No. 18, Pitlochry, now a clothing shop, was Tulls the Confectioner. At Christmas and Easter, Mr Tull made scenes of people and animals in chocolate. These were quite large and nearly filled the window. It was a feature of the town that the locals awaited eagerly each year.

Looking down River Street on the left was the old Italian Quarter before it became derelict and was subsequently demolished to make way for the car park.

At the top of River Street, opposite the Castle walls was Reeves the Butcher, premises now occupied by The Don Beni Pizzeria. Between Reeves and the Theatre Royal at no. 31 were the offices of Meux Brewery, one of many in the town in the early 1900s. Passing the Theatre Royal and on to the corner is no37. This was one of William Creek's shops and sold antiques and old books. Crossing the road, and just outside the gate that leads to the 'Hundred Steps' (actually there are 138) that climb steeply to the Castle above, was a horse trough. This was removed many years ago.

Heading towards the town centre while climbing the steep hill beneath the Castle wall and Curfew Tower, metal hoops can be seen in the gutter. After the horses had been watered at the bottom of the hill, those who needed to stop on the hill itself could do so in safety and comfort when the rear wheels of the wagon were wedged against a hoop, preventing it from rolling backwards.

Early in the 1900s, when horse transport was still evident in Windsor, HorseBrakes, Growlers and Flys plied their trade from the hill, especially at times such as Royal Ascot Races. These hoops would have been an asset for those waiting for fares. Today, the occasional horse-drawn carriage can be seen waiting to give tourists a short pleasure ride. Today however, these usually start at the top of the hill opposite the Harte and Garter Hotel where the road is level.

Having now reached the statue of Queen Victoria, and standing with your back to the Castle, look across to the Royal Windsor Information centre. This building used to be a tearoom called the Windlesora. Behind you and to your left is a shop called Culpepper. This is the surname of the proprietor, a herbalist by profession. At one time a coffee bar called the Tartan Room occupied these premises. A little further along, before you reach Market Cross House and the Town Hall, the shop on the corner of Queen Charlotte Street is called Woods and was a chemists. It is now Wood's Perfumery of Windsor. It had a reputation second to none and is now a world-renowned shop. Queen Charlotte Street is reputed to be the shortest in England (only 51ft 10" long and boasting only one front door). When reaching the Town Hall, previously known as the Corn Exchange, you will see that the central pillars do not actually reach the roof, but are free-standing. At the time of construction, and to keep the authorities quiet, they were put in place to alleviate the fear that the floor above might collapse. The actually serve no other purpose than being pleasing to the eye.

With your back to the statue, but this time looking down Peascod Street, on the right hand side, outside Barclays Bank, there used to be a Police box on a post. This contained a telephone from which a policeman on the beat would report back to the Police Station every hour. When traffic became heavy (bearing in mind the Peascod Street was open to traffic in both directions then) the duty officer would don white gloves and armbands and stand in the middle of the road with his back to the statue controlling traffic with a precise series of arm movements.

The drinking trough in front of the entrance to the Hundred Steps

The first shop on the eastside (left) of Peascod Street was Montague Burton the tailors, now Bally Shoes. No 5 was a small shop called A Ginger, which was a 'Ham and Beef' store – an early type of delicatessen but with much less variety than can be found in today's delicatessens. Next door was another branch of Reeves the Butchers which has now become Hinds the Jewellers. If you look above the shop front, there is still a caste of a cow's head on the façade of the building.

At this point, the Acre Passage leading to Madeira Walk and the Acre leads off Peascod Street from the left hand side

No 16 was Freeman, Hardy and Willis, a shoe shop. Two businesses, Body Shop and Accessorise now occupy these premises

No. 22 was Hill & Son an ironmongers and is now InterSports.

No. 29, Timothy Whites the chemist is now Dorothy Perkins.

Here is Peascod Place, which leads off the street to the left and towards the new library and telephone exchange

No. 31, the shop on the corner of Peascod Place, was MacFisheries and is now Levis.

No. 37, Curry's the Cyclemakers is now Boots Opticians.

No. 40, Bakers the Chemist and another William Creek's shop is now the Post Office.

William Street leads to Victoria Street on the left.

No. 42 on the corner of William Street was Wellmans the Ironmongers. This is where all the tradesmen went to buy their tools and components. It was reputed that if Wellmans didn't have it, then it was not available. This shop is now occupied by Millets Camping.

No. 46 was John Bright the Tailor. Much to my parent's horror and embarrassment, this is where I was measured for my first suit at the age of 16 (and for the first time without their guidance). Italian was the fashion at the time. I chose a pinstripe three button jacket with narrow, close cut trousers without turn-ups. I thought I looked the cat's whiskers, but a t a height of six foot four and a half, my parents were aghast at the comments of their friends and neighbours. I had this suit for years, even after I was married. It was a couple of years later that my wife told me how much she hate it and dreaded me turning up to meet her wearing that suit when we were courting. It was years later when looking back at some old photographs that I realised how totally unsuitable for a lad of my size it was, but boys will be boys, won't they?

Nos. 55/56 were a Tescos Store and are now Kitchen Kapers.

No. 69 housed the British and Argentine Meat Co. and is now Castle Fruiterers.

Here is Cross's Corner

The seed merchant called Cross, on the corner of St Leonard's Road and Clarence Road which was opposite the Old Criterion public house, always had a decorative seed display In the window. This was achieved by making a geometric pattern with coloured seeds and pulses against the inside of the shop window. This was about two feet high and extended the full width of the window. From time to time, when the various colours faded having been exposed to sunlight through glass, it was replaced with new seeds and a different pattern.

Crossing the road to the Old Criterion Pub and walking back along Peascod Street (west side), numbers 74-76 were a well-known grocers called David Gregg. All the staff in this shop wore a white shirt with tailored

Oxford Road before Ward Royal was built looking from Peascod Street

Oxford Road now

collar and a tie, a long blue and white striped apron, and a straw boater hat. Altogether they were extremely smart. Every thing was cut to order; I remember a large hand driven slicing machine standing on one of the marble topped counter. Cheese was cut from large blocks with a cheese wire. Butter was expertly shaped into the required amounts from twenty-eight or fifty-six pound blocks using two wooden spats, before being wrapped in greaseproof paper. Loose tea came in large chests and was measured and professionally wrapped in paper formed into a cone. This cone was hand filled with loose tea and the top turned down to make a packet. While being served, each item was priced by writing on the packet. When your purchases were complete, the assistant would pack your basket for you, totalling the items as he did. With a clunk, and the sound of the bell from the manual till and a 'Thank you for your custom Madam', the manager would often walk you to the door and hold it open for you while exchanging pleasantries. He would then bid you good day. This building is now occupied by Sketchley's the Dry Cleaners and the Dispensary for Sick Animals.

Nos. 79/80 was occupied by Bye the Stationers and Newsagent and is now Campsie the Estate Agent and Escape the Hairdressers.

No. 85 was another well known grocery store called Perk's Store and is now Kall Kwik Printers.

No. 86, Denny's the Bakers is now the Oxfam shop.

At this point Oxford Road leads off left towards Ward Royal.

No. 90 was Holmes' Fish Restaurant. My parents used this shop regularly. I remember sitting in the open cubicles with high-backed wooden seats. Included in the price of fish and chips was a slice of buttered bread and a cup of tea.

No. 93 was Darvilles the Grocer. This company still trades around the area. This shop is now Dolphin and Moben Kitchens.

No. 94 was another grocers called World Stores and is now Warwicks Mens Fashions.

No. 98, the Wellington public house is now the Café Prima. This drinking house was a favourite of the military who were billeted in Windsor.

No. 103, Edwards the Tobacconist and newsagent always had a large selection of pipes and tobacco, and a wide range of lighters. This site is now occupied by Savoy Tailors Guild, clothiers.

No 104 was the Duke of Cambridge public house. This was immediately next to the walk through called Creek's Cut. This was partially an archway formed by the shops in Peascod Street. On leaving the archway on the right were a few small shops. One of these was Midgeons the Tailors. This small walkway was known as Sydney Place. The Duke of Cambridge public house, and the shop on the other side of the cut called William Creek had their main entrances on Peascod Street. Over the years, Creek's shop expanded

Peascod Street in the early 1900s

Peascod Street in the late 1990s

Star and Garter Hotel

to take in nos. 105-111. The entrance to King Edward court now covers the area where nos. 104-111 once stood. This wide walkway is now flanked by Ernest Jones the Jewellers on the left and Rymans the Stationers on the right.

Just about where Clinton's Card Shop is now situated was another covered walkway leading to the Windsor Laundry. In it's heyday, this business employed about 80 workers.

No. 112 was Dexter's the Bakers. This was a small shop, only one room wide and three deep, with the back room housing the actual bakery. It produced all the old English produce such as Lardy Cakes, Penny Buns, Bath Buns, Jam Tarts and Slab Cake along with many varieties of bread no longer to be found. The smell wafting into Peascod Street was wonderful and there was always a long queue out into the street, whatever the time of day.

No. 113 was the Regal Cinema, one of three in the town and nicknamed 'The Fleapit'. This site is now occupied by a store called Next. Almost opposite was another cinema called the Empire.

Nos. 114/15 Lipton's the Grocers and Harris the Tobacconists have now become the River Island Trading Co.

The three shops that replaced the Star and Garter Hotel. Goswell Hill starts to the right of these three shops and is now a walkway to Windsor Central Station

No. 120, the Windsor and Eton Dairy Shop, had a rear entrance that led to the bottling plant and depot. The main access to this was in Goswell Lane. The dairy advertised that the milk came from their own pedigree Guernsey herd at Flemish Farm in Windsor Great Park. This shop is now part of the business called GAP.

Nos. 121-124 were absorbed by Daniel's Department Store. One of these small shops was called Home and Colonial Stores, another of Windsor's grocers at the time.

In recent times Daniel's store had been extended even more. It is now a large department store with three floors and boasting two eateries.

No. 130 is still occupied by Marks and Spencers and also now has two sales floors.

No. 131 was The Star and Garter Hotel with its infamous gymnasium at the rear. Such boxers as Sugar Ray Robinson trained here when preparing for a fight in England. Hush Puppy, Castle Pharmacy and Our Price now occupy this site.

Here is Goswell Hill

Goswell Hill starts to the right of the pictures on pages 81 and 82 and leads to the Windsor Central Station and Goswell Hill. This narrow hill is still cobbled. The cobbles are raised on alternate rows across the hill. This was to enable the horses to gain a grip on the steep gradient when climbing to the goods yards at the top from the gasworks below. Immediately opposite the sidings was a timber merchant called Priors. I used to collect sawdust for the butchers shop from this yard.

No. 135, Tulls the Bakers is now H. Samuel the Jewellers. Also on this site was Findlay & Co, a tobacconists. This shop specialised in products for smokers. It always carried a huge selection of loose tobacco in jars and a magnificent variety of pipes and accessories such as spills and pipe cleaners. It also sold snuff.

Above the tobacconists was a gentlemen's hairdressers owned by a Mr Frank Burton who passed away while serving his term as mayor in 1972. 'Ginger Burton', as he was affectionately known, was one of the instigators of the Windsor Open Air Swimming Pool. He fought hard to get this built, and it was opened, much to his satisfaction, in 1962. The original swimming baths were situated by the side of the small children's funfair. This was a backwater and is now used for the mooring of small pleasure craft. The men used to swim on the Castle side of the railway viaduct and the women and children on the other side. The concrete edging that formed the side of the baths can still be seen on this part of the river. The flat above the hairdressers was occupied by one of the Higley family. They owned and worked in the Monumental Stonemasons at 22 Alma Road. This yard was lost when the Ward Royal complex was built. Further along Alma Road, and after crossing Arthur Road on the right is the house that the Camm family lived in. Their firstborn, one of twelve children, became Sir Sidney Camm of Hurricane Aircraft fame.

Retracing your steps a few yards, when standing at the crossroads looking across Arthur Road, slightly to the left was the General Store owned by the Camm family. Next door to that was Thomas & Sons scrap merchants. It was here that the Windsor Liberal Rifle Club sold the lead retrieved from the target area of their range.

Briefly returning to Peascod Street and nearly reaching the top of the hill was No. 140, Elliott the Bootmaker. These premises are now occupied by Jones the shoe shop. A few more yards and you arrive back at the Queen Victoria statue and the main entrance to the Castle.

Statue of Queen Victoria who looks down Peascod Street

Chapter Eight - The Lean Years

The common working week in 1947/9 consisted of 45-52 hours. My father, a skilled carpenter and joiner worked a five and a half day week for a basic wage of £8 10s 6d before deductions. A student nurse's pay was £2 8s 0d but this shortly rose to £3 8s 5d. When I started my own apprenticeship as a cook in 1955 I received £2 5s 0d per week. The second year it rose to £2 7s 0d and the fifth year £4 17s 6d.

My working day consisted of nine hours split - four in the morning and five in the evening. This was for five days a week. On the sixth day, I attended technical college, but in the evening I was expected to work five hours. During the college holidays, I worked six days of nine-hour split shifts. I very rarely finished on time as the hotel restaurant did not close its doors until the shift ended and even then, latecomers were very rarely refused. The cleaning up then had to be completed before asking permission to leave the kitchen. If you wanted to eat a meal, it was in your own time. The nine hour days regularly became ten or eleven hours before you could get a bite to eat for yourself, and that was only if there was anything left over from the menu. My holiday entitlement was two week per year after one complete years service.

In this last chapter, I have put together some examples of the cost of living during the immediate post-war years, taking into account that many items were on ration. Below is a table of old currency to help put into perspective the prices of yesteryear when compared to today's currency.

Old Money

4 Farthings	1 Penny
2 Halfpennies	1 Penny
12 Pennies	1 Shilling
20 Shillings	1 Pound
240 Pennies	1 Pound

Abbreviations

PPPW	Per person, per week
R	Rationed
PTS	Points
QTY	Quantity

Basic Food Prices

Key: PPPW = Per Person per Week
       R = Rationed

BASIC FOOD INDEX

ITEM	R	QTY	PTS		COST
Sugar		lb			£0 0s 5d
Milk	R	PT	2.5-3.5/PT	PPPW	£0 0s 5d
Cheddar Cheese	R	lb	1$^1/_2$oz	PPPW	£0 1s 11d
Butter		lb			£0 1s 4d
Tea (loose)		$^1/_4$ lb			£0 0s 8$^1/_2$d
Back Bacon	R	lb	1oz	PPPW	£0 2s 0d
Large Eggs (broken ones replaced by law)		EA			£0 0s 3$^1/_2$d
Sweets (Spangles)	R	EA	5oz	PPPW	£0 0s 3d
Potatoes	R	lb	3lb	PPPW	£0 0s 2d
Bread (loaf)		2lb			£0 0s 10d
Flour		lb	3lb		£0 0s 9d
Jam (imported)	R	TIN (2lb)	(3pts)		£0 2s 10d
Oatmeal	R	lb	2pts		£0 03 3$^1/_2$d
Pork Sausages	R	TIN	2pts		£0 2s 10d
Diced Chicken/Turkey	R	TIN	20pts		£0 7s 0d
Slab Cake (Fruit)		lb			£0 1s 9d
Wedding Cake 1 Tier		EA			£3 5s 0d
Wedding Cake 2 Tier		EA			£4 15s 0d
Dried Prunes	R	lb	8pts		£0 0s 10d
Welgar Shredded Wheat		PKT			£0 0s 7d
Tinned Bacon Rashers		TIN	24 pts		£0 3s 0d
Brooke Bond Coffee *		BOT			£0 0s 11$^1/_2$d
Broken biscuits		lb			£0 1s 4$^1/_2$d
Beef Sausages (fresh)		lb			£0 1s 3d

* $^1/_2$d reclaimable upon return of the empty bottle

LEISURE

ITEM	COST
Cider (2 pints)	£0 1s 9d
Beer (1 pint)	£0 1s 4d
Cigarettes (Richmond 10 untipped)	£0 1s 2d
Cigarettes (Richmond 20 untipped)	£0 2s 4d
Suitcase	£1 2s 6d
Windsor & Eton Express newspaper (limited to 4 pages)	£0 0s 3d
Whiskey(bottle)	£0 17s 6d

TRANSPORT

ITEM	COST
Second-hand Bicycle	£2 0s 0d
Bus trip Windsor to Dedworth	£0 0s 2d
Coach trip Windsor to Brighton (return)	£0 7s 0d
Taxi (per mile to anywhere)	£0 0s 8d
Flight (London - Dublin return)	£11 0s 0d
Car - MG 1.25l (inc. purchase tax)	£671 11s 8d
Car - Austin 12c (inc. purchase tax)	£597 0s 0d
Road Fund License per year (each motorist limited to 90 miles per month)	£10 0s 0d

ACCOMMODATION

ITEM	COST
Rent 2 bedroom house or bungalow per week	£0 15s 6d
Buy 4 bedroom house in central Windsor with 2 reception rooms, kitchen, bathroom and garden (freehold)	£2250 0s 0d

CLOTHES AND ACCESSORIES

ITEM	COST
Ladies topcoat	£5 4s 3d
Blouse	£3 17s 6d
Handbag	£1 3s 4d
Children's coat and hat set	£2 4s 7d
Ladies sandals	£0 15s 5d
Boys/Girls shoes	£0 13s 2$^{1}/_{2}$d
Man's suit	£18 4s 6d
Man's sports jacket	£5 15s 0d
Fully fashioned Bemburg hose stockings	£0 13s 11d

NOTE: Ladies were urged not to go for the new longer fashions and stay with shorter skirts to save on cloth. Clothes rationing finished by 1949.

ENTERTAINMENT

ITEM	COST
Royal Windsor Horse Show - seats at	£0 2s 6d
	£0 5s 0d
Entrance fee	£0 1s 0d
Saturday morning pictures	£0 0s 6d
Aspro Nicolas Christmas pantomime	£0 2s 6d
	£0 3s 6d
	£0 5s 0d
	£0 7s 6d
London Football match (terraces)	£0 0s 6d
ABC Cinema Restaurant (lunch and pudding)	£0 3s 0d
Lyons Corner House Restaurant (Meat pie & chips, apple pie & custard & coffee)	£0 4s 0d
Olive Branch (near Theatre Royal) restaurant Windsor (lunch)	£0 3s 0d
Theatre Dinner	£0 3s 6d
New Year's Eve Dance (entrance)	£0 3s 6d
New Year's Eve Gala Dinner	£0 15s 0d
Old House Hotel Christmas Day dinner and film show	£0 12s 0d

Ration Books were a must for everyone

HOUSEHOLD

ITEM	COST
Blankets (surplus wartime) (double)	£0 8s 4d
Radio - Phillips 4 valve L/M/S	£19 8s 8d
Oak dining room table and 4 chairs	£18 6s 9d
Oak bedroom suite	£79 10s 0d

GENERAL

ITEM	COST
Football pools, top dividend £50,382. Stake	6d
Plus per season for paper control	2s 0d
Shoe repairs, sole and heel	£0 10s 6d
Old age pension per week	£1 4s 0d
Eton College fees per year + games subscription	£308 0s 0d £10 0s 0d

Looking back over those early years, and comparing the way of life with the one that we have today, I sometimes feel those hard times, together with the consideration and respect people had for the law and each other, were more desirable than the modern, and rather selfish, throw away society that we live in today.

I am currently researching a second book called *The World At My Feet*. The story begins by telling of the experiences of a young teenager starting work in the hostile environment of a hotel kitchen in 1954.

It goes on to tell of my travels around the world on an ocean liner in the mid 60's, what life was like living on a South Sea island for six years, and upon returning to 'Dear Old Blighty', it describes the shock of discovering just how so much had changed in such a short period of time. It then describes life in England during the 70s and 80s, and finally of the joys of living in a small pocket of rural England at the turn of the century – although being within easy reach of the international airport at 'Heathrow', numerous motorways and the largest industrial estate in the south of England. Despite all this the area still retains its lush riverside water meadows which support an abundance of wildlife. It also has an ambience that was taken for granted in the early and middle years of the 1900s.

THAMESWEB
Windsor

The Windsor Web Site

www.thamesweb.co.uk/windsor/

An ever growing resource for Windsor past and present.

We welcome your stories, photos and histories.

Tel: 01753 620540

Email: editor@thamesweb.co.uk